Introduction

"Education is not filling a bucket, but lighting a fire."
—William Butler Yeats

When I first decided to become a teacher, I was far more interested in my subject area (history) than in students. My student-teaching experience helped change that for me. I quickly learned that education has everything to do with the consumer, and little to do with the purveyor.

I've also learned that although quite a lot of education takes place in school, opportunities for education are hardly exclusive to the classroom. What's more, it's not just school children who learn.

You hold in your hand a collection of true stories that work a common theme: the ability of education to change a life forever. Not all of them take place in a conventional classroom, and not all of the experiences involve a teacher changing the life of a student. Sometimes it's vice-versa. Sometimes it's an experience that goes both ways. Heck, sometimes the student *becomes* the teacher.

It's experiences like these that so often remind me that I have the best job in the world.

What these stories share is the notion that education matters, that "teaching moments" can arise anywhere, at any time. What's more, the authors who have poured their own experiences into these stories have all helped bring home to the reader the notion that participating in the educational process is in many ways the defining moment of the human condition. Put simply: learning is about being *human*.

Think about it. If you want to find someone who is still learning, take a look around you. If you want to find someone who isn't, try a cemetery.

Teacher Miracles celebrates that process, and more, it celebrates those participants. I am so proud to have had a small part in putting this book together. I am even prouder to have my name associated with those of the authors who worked so hard to give their experiences life again, to tell their stories, and to share a bit of learned wisdom, a laugh, or a tender, unforgettable moment with you, the reader.

In truth, I am humbled by these authors. I am grateful for their dedication, their persistence, their patience with the sometimes tedious editing process, and their moments of glad grace when helping me put the finishing touches on this shared labor of love.

I hope that you enjoy these stories. Moreover, I hope that you learn something from them.

Goodness knows that I have.

Brian Thornton

Teacher Miracles

INSPIRATIONAL TRUE STORIES
FROM THE CLASSROOM

Edited by Brian Thornton

ADAMS MEDIA
Avon, Massachusetts

Published by
Adams Media, an F+W Publications Company
57 Littlefield Street, Avon, MA 02322. U.S.A.
www.adamsmedia.com

ISBN 10: 1-59869-135-X
ISBN 13: 978-1-59869-135-1

Printed in the United States of America.

J I H G F E D C B A

Library of Congress Cataloging-in-Publication Data
available from the publisher

This publication is designed to provide accurate and authoritative information with regard to the subject matter covered. It is sold with the understanding that the publisher is not engaged in rendering legal, accounting, or other professional advice. If legal advice or other expert assistance is required, the services of a competent professional person should be sought.
　　　　　　　　　　—From a *Declaration of Principles* jointly adopted by a Committee of the American Bar Association and a Committee of Publishers and Associations

Many of the designations used by manufacturers and sellers to distinguish their products are claimed as trademarks. Where those designations appear in this book and Adams Media was aware of a trademark claim, the designations have been printed with initial capital letters.

While all the events and experiences recounted in this book are true and happened to real people, some of the names, dates, and places have been changed in order to protect the privacy of certain individuals.

The poems featured in "Staying Gold" (*How It Started, My Apology,
Perpetrator, My Monster,* and *In the Moment*) have been used with permission
of Vanessa Ragains.
Cover images ©Bart Harris and ©Glen Jones

*This book is available at quantity discounts for bulk purchases.
For information, call 1-800-289-0963.*

Of Magellan and the Bottom of the World

By Natalie Lorenzi

*M*iguel saunters into my classroom in his baggy jeans and white T-shirt, trailed by the other five sixth graders who come to me for help with English. Like Miguel, the other boys don't walk anywhere—they swagger. The girls' eyes peek out from underneath blue eye shadow and mascara that's too thick—girls on the verge of becoming women.

All six students moved to the United States from Central America at least four years ago, but they lag an average of three academic years behind their peers. In their regular classrooms, none of these kids can keep up, and they know it. Long ago they learned to label themselves as "stupid" or "slow." But here, they take refuge in the haven of my

English as a Second Language class. When they come through my door, they visibly shed the bravado that camouflages their desperation to succeed in a society that denies them full membership. Here, under my tutelage, they can finally shine.

Gathered with my adolescent charges around a U-shaped table, I begin a lesson on Ferdinand Magellan, one of the more colorful explorers of his time. My eyes widen and my voice drops as I weave the tale of five ships, braving choppy waters and howling winds to round the southern tip of South America.

Jaime leans in to catch my words.

Each ship has its own captain, but Magellan commands them all. As the ships near the desolate tip of the continent, word of a nascent mutiny reaches Magellan. Keeping this information to himself, he signals the ships to pull over. The crew disembarks, and stands on the shores of Tierra del Fuego—a wild land, to be sure.

Arturo's eyes grow wider. "What's he gonna do, Mrs. Lorenzi?"

"Magellan reveals that he knows of the plot against him," I say. "He observes the mutinous captains as they shift their glances and their weight from one foot to the other. Then, without warning—Magellan decapitates two of the traitors!"

Melissa looks down at her folded hands.

"Magellan barks the order to board the ships and prepare to set sail," I tell them, "abandoning a third captain and a traitorous priest in this inhospitable land to fend for themselves."

I pause for dramatic effect—I know I've got them hooked. This is the stuff of which teaching is made—bringing history to life, raising it to a level on par with Hollywood's silver screen. Whatever these kids missed from their history textbooks, I will fill in the blanks for them now. I'll make them love history, love learning, and perhaps love themselves.

Miguel folds his arms, shakes his head and leans back in his chair, stretching his legs out before him. "Man, if I was those other captains, I just would have kicked Magellan's you-know-what."

"Right, Miguel," I say. "You've just seen two men get their heads lopped off—don't you think you'd be a little scared? I'm not talking about the movies, here. I'm talking about witnessing this in *real* life, you know—right before your eyes!"

"We know." Edwin shrugs.

Miguel shakes his head. "Man, when they cut off someone's head, you can't show you're scared. That's what they want."

"Yeah," Melissa says. "Like even when they make the whole village come and see it, and the man's wife is holding their baby and crying on her knees and begging them not to do it. Man, they do it anyway. They don't care."

I stare at them, my mouth open. What are they talking about?

"Mrs. Lorenzi—you never saw someone's head get cut off, did you?" Ana punctuates her question with a slight lift of her chin.

I pause, my eyes scanning for a mischievous grin, a raised eyebrow—any signal that the joke is over. Nothing. Are they serious? Their eyes wait for my answer—somber, with memories flashing behind them like gunfire. They aren't kidding.

"No." I lean forward, my chin propped on my fist. "I've never seen anyone get their head cut off."

"Man," Miguel says, shaking his head again, forcing his lips into a crooked, half-smile. "I hope you never do, Mrs. Lorenzi." He shrugs shoulders, despite the weight they carry. "I hope you never do."

As if they'd all come to some silent agreement, they nod their heads, eyes cast downwards. Like parents who think their kids can't handle the news that the family dog has just died.

Somehow I stumble through the rest of the lesson. I focus on Magellan's accomplishments, sidestepping the starvation, scurvy, and murder for today. The group works in silence and actually follows every direction that I give. They finish their assignments in record time.

They rise with the sound of the bell, gather their book,s and shuffle to the door, reluctant to leave this place where they all understand each other.

An hour ago, I thought that six children had filed into my classroom. How easily I am fooled. They are actually six adults, masquerading as adolescents with their American clothes and American slang. They are adults, decades older than I, old souls who have witnessed the pummeling of their lush, beautiful countries by death squads and war and guerrillas and poverty. They spill out into the hallway, calling, "See ya, Mrs. Lorenzi," their masks of indifference set firmly in place once again.

Who am I to be teaching them?

I Love You, Too, Charlie

By Catherine K. March

*C*rash, the reading clinic door burst open and they came bounding into the room. Four pint-sized individuals from Miss Bisbratt's first-grade class, each intent on being first.

Somebody was missing. It was Charlie, of course—who else would it be? Charlie never missed school, but he sometimes missed reading class. "It's fun," he said. Even though he knew that reading was not easy for him.

"Good morning," I said. "I'm glad you're here. NOW, sit down and collect yourselves. Is Charlie not in school today?" I already knew the answer.

"Charlie's in trouble." This from Amanda, a tiny, red-haired child with a conspicuous overbite and an even more conspicuous attitude. "Miss Bisbratt says he don't follow directions."

Ah yes, I well knew Charlie's trouble with directions. Whether deliberately thought out or whether the result of a genetic inability to comprehend them or because he deliberately avoided listening, I was not sure. Nobody had nailed the problem down yet. And to Miss Bisbratt's despair, after three and one-half months Charlie still could not "make his name." I had attempted to encourage her that there was hope for him, but we never quite saw eye-to-eye on the subject.

Ever since September that year, I, a reading specialist by training, had been expected to spend my allotted forty minutes a day with each class, first through third, teaching math and reading to children who cared not a fig about either. What they wanted was the playground and lunch.

They came from the trailer parks that surrounded this small Ohio town and every classroom teacher was certain from the start that they would never learn to read, write, or cipher well enough to pass the proficiencies no matter how long they were in school. As the resident reading specialist, I was their only chance for deliverance and sometimes I felt sadly unequal to the task.

My heart went out to them, these kids, because society seemed to have pigeonholed them as unreachable. In my heart, I knew they were not. Most of them needed only extra time and extra care and a chance to stay in one place for a while. For whatever reason, many a family just hitched their truck up to the trailer and moved on to what they must have hoped would be a better opportunity for life. They were not unlike the migrants of the '30s, moving from one place to another in search of something. Had the American Dream run out on them?

Charlie was personally acquainted with this phenomenon.

"I went to see Missy on Sunday and she wasn't home. Even her house was gone." His blue eyes registered distress and lack of comprehension.

"Oh, they just took their trailer and moved out." Amanda raised her eyebrows at such innocence.

Charlie had also been in three different schools since kindergarten, leaving him with a fragmented introduction to learning. In addition, he was a small child, in constant motion, swinging his feet, skipping when he should have walked, dropping his lunch pail on the bus. His attention was so scattered that during quiet reading time he sometimes sat flipping the pages of his book at a tremendous rate.

"What are you doing?" I asked.

"Reading." He smiled up at me.

I was not sure Miss Bisbratt would agree. She had filled me in on her perception of trailer park kids when first we met.

"I always check where the children come from," Miss Bisbratt told me. "When I make up my reading groups, the low group always comes from the trailer parks and they stay in the low group all year."

I'll just bet they do, I thought to myself.

Though Charlie was doomed to be in Miss Bisbratt's room, he actually spent more time in the hall than in his classroom. Out there, he learned little about reading, writing, or math, but he did learn to mark up the door with a crayon he had stowed away in his pocket. He seemed to love crayons no matter whether they were whole, broken, or what color. Now, here he was, with Christmas looming on the horizon, in trouble again, and missing the fun.

It was the first week of December, and in an effort to correlate reading and math skills, I had used counting books with the children. *The Twelve Days of Christmas* seemed perfect with *A Visit from St. Nicholas* as an added bonus. We drew and counted eight tiny reindeer prancing and sugar plums dancing and it was good because most of them knew how many and could write the numbers on the bottom of the paper under their names. I felt some certainty about their possible improvement.

Still, Charlie never quite got the picture. His reindeer numbered anywhere from three to fifteen, even after several tries. His sugar plums danced, but he couldn't tell how many to save his life, even though we tried it time and again. I was not surprised that he hadn't followed Miss Bisbratt's directions.

"Let's get on with our lesson," I told my "Reluctant Readers." "I'll see about Charlie."

I left the mother helper who volunteered once a week in the Reading Clinic to supervise the counting and drawing of a partridge in a pear tree, and went down the hall to Miss Bisbratt's room. Miss Bisbratt turned Charlie loose with much reluctance.

"Charlie has four do-overs," she said, her tone unnecessarily grim. "He'll be inside for recess today getting those worksheets done."

She was still sputtering when I closed the door, taking the criminal with me. I decided to get his attention for today's lesson right away.

"Charlie," I said. "The others are drawing a picture of a partridge in a pear tree. You remember our story this week? Do you think you can do that?"

Charlie nodded.

"Do you remember how many partridges there were?"

"One."

"And how many pears on the tree?"

"Three."

"And do you remember what a partridge is?"

"Bird."

There was none of the usual familiar chatter from a naturally lively child. The little feet did not skip. He held my hand.

Everybody was deep in their pear trees when we got back. Even Amanda did not look up from her masterpiece. I settled Charlie in a chair at the table with the rest, gave him drawing paper and crayons, whispered the lesson in his ear one more time and moved to look at the others. For a moment or two, silence hung over the room. My mother volunteer and I exchanged smiles, and she went back to arranging books in the reading corner.

"That ain't what you're 'sposed to do." Amanda's accusing voice cracked the stillness.

Charlie looked up. "Leave me be."

Then I saw his picture. Christmas trees marched across the page while Santa, in a lopsided sleigh, sailed with his motley collection of reindeer across a sky filled with bright green stars. Once again, our Charlie had marched to the beat of his own drummer.

Amanda saw my despairing expression.

"Oh," she said, her voice irritable. "Just take his crayons away from him. That's what Miss Bisbratt does.

Amanda, I thought, *you are getting to be a lot like Miss Bisbratt.* I did not take away his crayons. Charlie shot her a triumphant look, and finished his picture.

He was the last to leave when the class was over. Standing there, shifting from one foot to the other, he shoved his picture at me. "I love you," he said.

"I love you, too, Charlie," I said. "Thank you." And I hung his picture on the bulletin board with all the others. He watched, not saying a word.

The last day before Winter Break, there was a knock at my door. I left my third graders and opened it to find Charlie with a paper in his hand. Amanda was with him.

"Teacher wouldn't let him go without me," she said. "She thinks he'll go home."

I thought that if I were Charlie I would go home, too.

Charlie rolled his eyes.

"I got somethin for you. You know why I to'ja I love ya?"

I shook my head.

Amanda opened her mouth.

"Let me tell 'er," Charlie ordered.

She stood back, surprised.

"It's cause you put up my picher anyhow and you din't take my crayons away."

He shoved the sheet of wrinkled, lined, notebook paper at me. On it was a dangerously tilted, brilliantly colored tree with three, skinny, yellow pears and a bright orange, distraught-looking partridge clinging to a purple branch. The numbers three and one were printed at the bottom beside his name.

"I done it myself," Charlie said. "Nobody helped me."

I got down next to the children, looking them right in the eyes.

"Great work, Charlie," I said. "And Amanda, you were kind to come with him. May I give you both a hug?"

Momentarily entangled in two sets of arms, I nearly wept at one of the best hugs I ever got. Charlie skipped all the way back to his classroom, with Amanda right beside him. I pretended I didn't see.

I don't know what happened to Charlie. He was in school until June, but in September, I heard that his family moved from the trailer park, taking their "house" with them. Amanda said she saw them go, but didn't get there in time to say goodbye.

"Goodbye, Charlie," I said. "Wherever you are, I love you, too."

Tales from the Best Music Teacher in the Universe!

By Marianne Forkin

*I*t was my first year teaching music. I was ecstatic and terrified; I felt like there was so much pressure to do everything just right. So, I was teaching my little first graders all about the families of instruments. It was one of the very first lessons I taught while student teaching and it earned me an A+.

I stood in front of the class and rattled off all about the Brass family, the kids seemed intrigued and I felt like I was the best music teacher in the universe.

Next came the Woodwinds. "What's this one?" I'd ask, and all of a sudden hands would fly up: "Flute!" one would say.

"Clarinet!"

"Saxophone!"

"Very good!" I looked up and down and smiled my widest smile.

We sailed through Percussion and were on to Strings when I went into detail about the cello. I talked about how much I loved the sound of it, the smoothness and tone it made. Such a beautiful instrument—I told them how I wished I had one to bring in.

A little girl with blonde, curly hair raised her hand—this was long before the time those faces grew names for me. At this point they were kid number one and kid number two, etc.

I called on her and was surprised by what she said, "I have a cello and I can bring it in."

I glanced up at the first-grade teacher. She looked perplexed.

"You do? Are you sure?"

The little girl nodded and smiled, "Yup, my mommy loves the cello too."

"Okay," I said, never expecting the issue to be brought up again.

A week later I walked into that classroom, already convinced I was the best music teacher ever to set foot in that school, when that little blonde girl walked over to me all excited. "I brought you my cello!" she said.

I immediately looked all around the room, then at the teacher, who shrugged at me. I was a little perplexed by how this child could bring in such a huge instrument, not only because she was so tiny she would be able to fit in the case, but also, how could it possibly go undetected by her teacher?

"You did?"

"Yup!"

"Well where is it?"

"It's in my backpack."

I was intrigued by that answer as she ran to her backpack and grabbed her cello out of the front pocket.

She walked up to me and proudly handed me the box. "I forgot to ask you what your favorite flavor was . . . " she said, "but we bought you cherry!"

I looked down at the box of Jello and smiled.

From then on, every time I think that I'm the best music teacher in the universe, I have another "Jello" moment. I still have that box of cherry Jello to this day. I keep it in my schoolbag to remind myself that kids are the best and I have a lot to learn.

Langston Learns to Write

By Jan Baker

*T*he warm autumn sunshine illuminated me and Mr. Havashawn as I slid the fat manila envelope across the post office counter. Honeysuckle bloomed by the open door and scented the room. I could hear the bells ringing the hour in the town square. Usually I was too busy at ten o'clock on a September weekday morning to enjoy pretty smells or sounds. Usually I taught English to a mob of high schoolers a half hour away in the city, as I had for thirty years. I felt guilty, like a kid playing hooky.

"So this is it, huh?" he smiled at me.

"Well, I crossed the t's and dotted the i's, and I guess it's all good, Morty," I answered, remembering the intricacies of pension structures and health care choices in the state retirement application. My completed application was in the envelope. It had eight pages full of boxes to check, blanks to fill in, and a place for your social security number on every page, like you already had to wear a name tag or you might forget. Together with the envelope and the paperclip, the postage would be a dollar eleven cents: $1.11. That seemed like a lucky number. I was prepared to think it made an auspicious beginning to a new life.

"It ain't easy bein' a school teacher these days. I guess you've earned a rest!" Mr. Havashawn brought me back to the moment. "Any regrets? Brags?"

"Lots of both, Morty, lots of both." Teaching is a hard job. It doesn't matter where you teach, or what age group. Teaching in a city high school brings special trials, sure—violence, funerals, and drugs were unfortunately realities I dealt with all the time. But if anybody asked me which student I'd remember best—it'd be a country boy, Langston Claywell.

Everybody knew Langston, because everybody was afraid of him. Langston was always simmering with quiet anger. He was from the country and talked like it, and he was intelligent enough to be embarrassed by it. Langston Claywell played football. He didn't actually play football very well, only second string. Every year since he was a freshman he'd gotten madder and bigger, everybody guessed steroids. He was always in trouble, always in the dean's office, and then there'd been some bad family problem, and he'd ended up in foster care, looking even poorer and scrubbier.

I remembered all that when I looked up the first day of school that year in August and saw him in the last seat by the windows in my senior third period.

All through class I thought about how I could get rid of him. As I described the coming year, I emphasized the worst. There were easier senior teachers, and instead of reassuring them that it would be worth it, I pushed negatives and pushed them hard, right at Langston, so he could get his counselor to switch him. "All work is rubric graded," I said. That meant it would be graded fairly, according to a tough set of indicators, instead of the way, say, Mrs. Smith down the hall usually graded them, after a couple of good stiff drinks to put the bloom upon the rose. "This could get tough," I said.

"In two semesters you will write eight papers of nine different kinds of writing. Two speeches, two short stories, a creative nonfiction, two poems, a how-to-do-it piece—each one with multiple drafts. This is more than most college classes. But the school board in its wisdom has set that number and that variety, and we by the grace of God will do it." Surely that would encourage Langston to seek out Mr. Healey in 210, who would recite poetry at him in his deep, authoritative voice, and then give him an essay cheat sheet where he could fill in a few blanks and copy the rest in his own handwriting and call it writing. He could get an A and his self-esteem would never quiver.

And it was okay if I didn't want him, I told myself. As ranking senior teacher, I was allowed. My state test scores were making the school look good. I used standards-based instruction, which involved the examination of model writings that I forced kids to take apart word by word until they understood why writers called it "good." Then I made them write one. And write it again until structurally it matched the model. Except that often it exceeded the model, because when kids with the rich life experience of most inner city kids are taught *how* to do it, they *rule*. It's just tough—what an understatement!—to get them to that place. Many teachers back off, and live.

Everybody in the building knew how hard this kind of intense instruction was on the teacher, and how one single kid bent on class disruption could wreck it. For years now all I had to do was say the word, and the worst of the worst, like Langston, appeared on someone else's roster. Those teachers didn't want them either, but they weren't willing to pay the price. Maybe they were wiser, in balance. I never had a lot left for a life at the end of the day. But my word at least had weight in the counseling office where the schedules were made.

So I wrote a little note at the end of that first day with Langston's name on it, along with eight others, and requested that my classes be balanced in size by reassigning these students, please. Perfectly reasonable, as my classes were oversize, and by union contract had to be balanced. Perfectly professional to give away a mix of kids, even one good kid. I always tried to play the game graciously.

The next day Langston was not in third period. We began our study of the first model. It demonstrated how to pack writing with sensory details and how to begin with a scene, with people talking. They had to learn a picky chore, how to punctuate dialogue. Kids took turns using the computer and projector to practice instead of the scarred old blackboard, and that softened the blow, since they liked the technology I always managed to get grant money to obtain. So I ended the second day late as usual, but satisfied. All the classes seemed teachable. *I guess I can pull it off again*, I thought, and grabbed my purse to go.

And somebody started to kick my door in. It was locked. We weren't supposed to lock the doors, but after hours, when security went home, I always locked mine. The kids coming for help had to knock to enter. Somebody had tried it, found it locked, and started battering. It was incredibly loud and scary, echoing in the empty building.

It was Langston. The door was hanging by one hinge, and his shoulder was wedged where there had been a glass pane in the top half. His face was wet. "You don't want me!" he shouted, and started to blubber. "You don't want me and you put my name on a list and they took me out!"

"Calm down, Langston. Here, back out. I can open it." In the interest of self-defense, I tried to stay calm, but my heart was pounding.

"Why don't you want me?" he shouted at me. "Ain't I as good as anybody else?" Fury mixed with tears.

"It's not that, Langston. My classes are too big. We have to take some kids out. I thought you might do better with somebody else who doesn't do all those required writings. You know, you have football practice."

"But no! I understand the way you do it. You teach the way Coach does. I get it. I want *you!*" He took a deep, shuddering breath and stopped crying. He tried to speak normally. "Please don't kick me out. You don't know me. But I can do it! Ask Coach! Everybody says you're nice, why can't you be nice to *me*?"

That stung. Why couldn't I? I looked at the broken door. I looked at the kid standing in front of me, who outweighed me by a hundred pounds and had broken that door down just because he was mad. I decided to forget the lecture on manners—whose were worse, his, or mine?

His words rang in my head. *You don't know me.* The evil, rotten kernel of injustice. *I am a person, but because of the color of my skin, or my accent, or my disability, or my ability, either one, you don't know me, and you don't want to, and you will make decisions for me and about me without knowing me, and it hurts the worst of anything.*

"Okay," I said. "Yeah. Okay." He'd out-argued me. What do we teach, if not honor?

He relaxed and pulled his shoulder out of the shattered door. He looked at me. "You won't be sorry."

"I'm not sorry now. I'm sorry I put you on the list. I'm sorry about that." I paused for minute and let the apology sink in. "You come to class tomorrow, I'll tell counseling. Help me figure out what to tell maintenance about the door."

He grinned gratefully, and wiped his face. "You could tell 'em I was just playing around. They used to me."

He kept his word. He listened in class. He came for help after football practice, every day. Every day he tried to outwork me, outlast me. I never had a student do that before, and began to feel more optimistic about the jumbled, misspelled, incoherent tangle of Langston's first writing sample. There's not much that hard work won't cure. I analyzed his writing for the error pattern, to find the error that most impeded understanding. Eighty-eight percent of Langston's errors were run-on sentences, and they caused his writing to be unintelligible because there were no stops to help the reader out. He had to learn commas and periods and semicolons, and re-work practically every sentence. He got it, not quickly, not easily, but he got it. Now he made sense. He seemed less angry.

Then we worked on his country dialect errors, not because they really impeded intelligibility, but because there is such prejudice against them. The first time, he literally gasped from the correction, and said, with a wounded glance, "That's how my gramma be sayin' it," like I had spit in the Holy Grail.

But I showed him how it's just two different dialects, not a right one or wrong one, just two different ones. Anybody can learn them both. Besides, you can still use Gramma's dialect, just inside of quotes. It's called dialogue. Then it's not only *not* wrong, readers love it. They give high scores for it on state tests, too, when it's punctuated correctly. "Look, let me show you." I showed him models, Langston Hughes and Ralph Ellison. He got it. It took several sessions. Five-thirty would roll around, six-thirty, no dinner, under the flickering fluorescents, the two of us trying to wear each other out: where does the comma go, where do you put the question mark, inside the quotes or outside? He kept coming. Meanwhile, they switched his foster home and he needed a haircut. But he still seemed less angry, calmer. Langston had a very nice smile and along with punctuation, he was using it more often.

Writing is two things, Langston, I told him. It's looking life right in the eye, and then putting it down on paper, no b.s. But I began to feel I was only teaching him the second half and maybe he was doing okay on his own for the rest. He kept coming.

Fall wore on. The football season was almost over. Time for the Big Game. Every high school has one, right? We hadn't beat Washington High in thirteen years. They were the elite inner city school, where they sent the kids who tested at grade level. They always beat us, at everything.

Except this year. The year I had Langston, we came from seventeen points behind and beat them in the last quarter. Langston got to play a lot, and I watched him get the snot knocked out of him and get up again and again, and I cheered myself hoarse. For something else. Because where does that come from, to keep getting up? You can't buy it. You can't force it. Every time we meet it, all we can do is cheer. The grace of my profession is that teachers get the chance to meet it so often.

He wasn't in third period the next day. He showed up after school.

"Look what I got," he said. It was his beat-up red plastic disk carrier. "Ms. Molino let me stay all day in the library—the *library*—for the computers. Did she tell you? She said she'd tell my teachers. I wrote about the game. It's nonfiction. Right?" He was trembling.

We put it up on the big monitor. He had the game, alright. Now I was trembling.

He started with a scene, just like the creative nonfiction model taught. His featured a snatch of breezy dialogue among the cheerleaders just at the start of the game that was authentic as hell. In the first paragraph, he put the reader *there*, using the senses. He had the band, and you could hear the music because he named the song. He had the smell of the place, the just-cut grass, the sweat, the hotdogs, some neighbor's burning leaves. He wove in specific pep team chants and catcalls from the crowd. He had dialogue from *inside* the huddle. It was in dialect, naturally, and he punctuated it *almost* perfectly and moderated the profanity—just enough to be family-friendly but fresh. He had what Coach said, just how Coach sounds, intermixed with play descriptions. He had the living, breathing heart of the game.

I told him how to submit it for publication, of course. It was accepted in the alumni newsletter, the school Web site, where it got the most hits ever, and even made the local newspaper's sports section. He earned a hundred bucks. Langston was a made man. Not at all the way we had expected.

Three years later, when Langston was a junior in college on a full scholarship, he came back to visit. He told me he was still using his high school writings, they were good enough for college English. That was after he picked me up off my feet in the parking lot and whirled me around and around. He was even larger than he had been in high school, but he wasn't angry anymore.

Mr. Havashawn was looking at me expectantly. "Yeah, Morty. Teaching was a good living. I think I've earned some time off."

"Go get 'em, girl," he said. He plopped the manila envelope into a mail bag. Done, it was done.

"Okay," I promised, and stepped out smiling into the bright autumn day.

Returning

By Kenneth Pobo

welve years ago, I shared an office with a history teacher in Loveland Hall, and had a desk that was a jumble of papers. Memos gathered dust under memos, their pleas carried off by the squirrels that sometimes leapt through the window seeking nuts.

"A poet in academia." From my graduate school time onward, I've wondered if that phrase is an oxymoron. I think of Allen Ginsberg trying to levitate the Pentagon as a protest against the Vietnam War. He swears it did levitate, just a bit.

I doubted if much levitation happened in any college. How can one rise when weighed down by papers or false smiles that make one shiver rather than take wing? Then I met Leah.

She was a seventy-three-year-old "returning adult student." Everything gets a category, a label. We had a short conversation in the hall. She knew I was the school poet (is this like being a mascot for a football team?) and said, "I can't write poetry."

"Yes, you can," I replied.

As we talked, an image of airplane flights came to me. Often someone plops down beside me and wants to talk. They ask the inevitable questions—where am I from? What do I do? When I say, "I teach English" I often get the same response: "Oh, I was always terrible in English." Am I to absolve them? I feel like a priest. Forgive me, father, for I have too many comma splices.

With Leah, I sensed that I'd see her again, perhaps in one of my classes. I didn't think our brief chat would be the end. The following fall I taught "Introduction to Poetry Writing" to mostly sophomores and juniors. There was Leah, in her pink dress, carrying a purse, the texts before her. Despite her statement that she couldn't write poetry, I wasn't surprised to see her there.

Each week I required students to turn in poems, some of which had to be written in traditional forms such as the sonnet and villanelle. Leah's poem was never late. Many of her poems were (and still are) about her family of origin or her own family or her struggles to become more educated. I wondered what kinds of comments would be most useful for her. My own glass of experience was filled quite differently from hers.

She's Jewish, a grandmother, a wife, someone who had a career in social work trying to help juveniles who got into trouble and had to face the courts. I was in my early forties. I grew up as a fundamentalist Protestant, a belief system I left in my twenties. I'm gay. I don't particularly enjoy being around children. Teaching matters to me—as does my interest in sixties pop music and gardens. And writing poetry.

Leah, even from that first class, has never enjoyed working in groups, preferring to consult with me in my office (now in "The English Suite" in the Kapelski Learning Center) about her work. Groups can be uncomfortable. It's hard to know what other writers can or will accept, what to say, what not to say. Even now, she's the same way.

I see her and her husband Shelley at the Sports Club, a local gym. Earlybirds, they arrive before I do, and when I see them on the treadmills I lug my gym bag, stuffed with student papers, a book I'm rereading for class, and my gym clothes, over to say hello. Shelley is proud of his wife. While many husbands thought it would be strange or embarrassing for a wife to want to work and to pursue a degree so she could work, he was supportive.

Now that Leah writes poetry, he remains supportive—as do her children. Her daughter Ethel gathers Leah's work together and prints it in attractive hardcover volumes called *Leaves of Greene*. Whitman would like the title. Leah's poems are green in that they sound and feel fresh, like new leaves on an oak. For Leah, poetry isn't about getting back youth, trying to mimic a collegiate voice. Poetry is a way into herself, and a way to connect with others. It's a territory where the map goes out of date five minutes after it's printed. The key to one poem won't unlock the next one. So she keeps working, refining her craft.

I've learned that easy compliments about her work will not satisfy her. Praise for its own sake rings hollow to her ears. Sometimes I don't have much to say about one of her poems—it seems pretty good—but I can always raise questions. Leah craves questions. She tussles with them, turns them around in her mind, lays the question out before each stanza and says, "What do I need to be thinking about, imagining, to improve this poem?"

At eighty-five, she's still taking classes. This semester she's enrolled in a course called The Writing Life and another about African art. A semester without Leah in class seems strange. She's been in many of mine, sometimes taking a particular one more than once. As a senior citizen not hunting for a degree, she doesn't have to write papers or take tests. She can do the assignments she wants to do.

I've had several senior students in various classes and have enjoyed most of them. Someone from an earlier generation can bring in a different view to a class discussion. If we study a poem about the Depression, I can include historical information, but Leah and the other senior students were there; they can make that time live for younger students in ways I can't. Yet it's not a one-way street. The younger ones contribute to the older ones too, bringing their experiences closer to the seniors' world.

Some days I go to school and think, "Another meeting, another class where too few are prepared." Discouragement slides in. Then Leah knocks on the office door. "Do you have some time? I have a couple of new ones." She hands them to me and I read her latest green(e) leaves. After we discuss them, she goes to her class, I to mine, and I'm ready to levitate.

Dancing for Dolmen

By Alexis Munier

*S*ince when do you dance?" Kati asked, stunned. In all our years of friendship I had declined most of her offers to go dancing, or would hide in the crowd, sipping my drink, praying silently that she wouldn't drag me out to the dance floor.

"Oh, I don't know, I guess I loosened up in Slovenia," I replied.

"I get it; you met some cute Slovene who finally got rid of your inhibitions." She smirked.

"Yeah, something like that." I smiled, remembering Dolmen.

Ten minutes before class was due to begin, Lidia rushed in carrying Dolmen in her arms. "Alexis, could we please have a chair with arms?" she scanned the small, modern classroom, "We don't want Dolmen to fall over!"

"Sure," I answered, making a mental note to rearrange the classroom furniture before every one of our weekly classes. Just as I struggled through the door with the over-size armchair, the other students began to arrive. Giggling at Dolmen, five years old but still carried "like a baby," the children shuffled in.

"Who's THAT?" demanded Kaya in Slovene.

"Everyone meet Dolmen, he's new to our class," I responded firmly. Not a peep from the other students.

Dolmen now tucked safely into his chair, his mother quietly left the room and we began class with our usual song. Not the least bit intimidated by the others, Dolmen immediately joined in and sang out loud and strong.

When I began teaching at a private language school in Maribor, Slovenia, I had imagined classes of young students repeating the alphabet in unison, listening eagerly to readings of *Green Eggs and Ham*. Instead I found teaching four- and five-year-olds consisted primarily of maintaining order, preferably in English. After a few months of classes I wasn't sure they had actually learned anything but "Stop that!" "Sit down!" or "That's enough!" Okay, they had learned a few basic swear words as well, for despite my best efforts there was an occasional slip of the tongue. But angels or demons, I seemed to be the only teacher willing to take on the kids' classes. I told myself the extra two euros an hour would make it worth my while in the long run, and pledged to have the kids speaking at least a few phrases by the end of the year.

Dolmen, despite his physical handicaps due to cerebral palsy, was my most gifted student. Well-behaved and disciplined, he would often reprimand the other students for goofing off and talking out of turn.

"Shhhh!" he'd say. "I'm learning English now!"

"Why are the other kids so bad, Alexis?" Dolmen asked me after class one day, as he waited for his mom to arrive.

"I don't know," I replied, knowing quite well that the other children would rather be jumping or playing than learning English. Jumping wasn't a possibility for Dolmen, who was in physical therapy in hopes of someday walking. For the moment, he crawled or depended on his parents to carry him where he wanted to go.

Despite an eagerness to learn, Dolmen was often absent. His condition left him susceptible to illness, and a severe cold could mean a week in the hospital. After missing a month of classes, his mother Lidia decided to pull him out.

"Please, Alexis," she asked me, "We would like to invite you over for dinner, to repay you for your kindness with Dolmen."

"Sounds great," I replied, and we made a date for Sunday evening.

With my poodle puppy, Oscar, in tow, I sat down to a delicious traditional dinner of beef stew and potatoes.

Lidia and her husband, Darko, were more than welcoming: opening ten-year-old wine and even serving a special dish of beef to Oscar. For the first time since I had arrived in Slovenia six months before, I felt at home. We talked and laughed, discussing everything from the recent addition of Slovenia to the E.U. to bad American pop music. Dolmen talked nonstop as well, in a mix of English and Slovene, with Lidia translating for me.

"So a Croatian, a Serbian, and the Pope walk into a bar . . . ," he began, the first of many "adult" jokes he delighted in telling that evening. After dinner, we moved to the comfortable living room.

"Mom!" he cried, "I want to play my music for Alexis!" Lidia put on his favorite CD of Slovene kids' songs, and Dolmen began to move. Rocking back and forth on his knees, he waved his arms in the air and shouted, "See, Alexis, this is how I dance!"

I stopped for a minute and tried desperately to hold back the tears. This little boy, unable to stand up or walk on his own, was dancing with all his heart.

"Alexis, dance with me!" he giggled, and I took his hands. On my knees with Dolmen, dancing for what seemed like an hour, the songs finally came to an end.

"Bedtime," Lidia said, "We've got to say goodbye to Alexis and Oscar now."

"Bye, Oscar," Dolmen said, patting his head. "Bye, Alexis," he whispered as he hugged me goodbye.

"Bye Dolmen, see you soon," I said as I made my way to the door. I didn't realize at the time that I would soon be leaving Maribor for Switzerland and as I walked out the door, walked completely out of their lives.

❀ ❀ ❀ ❀

Now and again, when the urge hits me, I dance. Usually in a club. Often in the kitchen. Sometimes I even kneel on the living room floor. Completely free, not a care in the world, I think back to before I met Dolmen. Always a little bit shy of my body, and not wanting to embarrass myself, I had avoided dancing for nearly thirty years. Not my friends, not my mother, not even my boyfriends had been able to make me dance. Only Dolmen, just four years old, had the power to inspire me.

Now, I've got to make up for lost time . . . .

Who Learned More?

By Patricia Harrington

*I*t was 1970, the waning days of the Civil Rights movement— and my first year of teaching.

My husband and I had returned to college two years before to get our degrees in education. We were both in our mid-thirties and wanted "regular" hours and more time to spend with our four children, ages one to ten. Teaching seemed an appropriate—and a worthwhile—way to accomplish those goals.

My first position after graduation was as a kindergarten teacher at Stanley Elementary School in Tacoma's Hilltop. Most of the families in the school's neighborhood were black and low income. As a result, the school was segregated. When friends learned of my assignment, they warned, "Stanley's a rough school. You don't want to teach there!" But then, the summer before my posting, the school district began a voluntary busing program. The district even initiated an innovative program that included a computer-skills lab at Stanley to attract non-minority students.

The district successfully integrated grades one through six, but the voluntary busing program didn't include kindergarteners. Consequently, on my first day of teaching, I faced twenty-three young, black students, some eager, others apprehensive. I went into the classroom to sing, "Mary Had a Little Lamb"; the children sent me out doing the "Funky Chicken."

In my growing-up years in Tacoma, my classes had students from all races. My high school cooking partner Rebina was African-American, and so was our student body president, Ben. We were friends, though not close, and I never gave any real thought as to whether I had any bias about other races. So I felt that I wouldn't have a problem teaching these five-year-olds from the heart of Tacoma's black community.

I must admit, however, that though a mother and thirty-five years old, I felt compelled as a new teacher to follow all of the techniques learned in my training. This was especially true in the early weeks of the school year. The course work didn't prepare me, however, for the real world of being with these children, all with different needs—and from a different culture.

The struggle to divide mother from teacher became more difficult, when our youngest son, Mikey, came down with a rare illness. He was only six at the time and the doctors had to run many tests on him in the hospital. They called it "conducting a differential diagnosis." It seemed at the time, that while I was trying to get my feet under me as a teacher, I was losing them—and the ground underneath me—as a mother. I couldn't hold Mikey, or press my cheek against his face and stroke his hair. His illness made all physical touch, even the weight of his bedsheets, painful. I could only caress him with whispered words of love.

The days ground on from September into October, and the children challenged me, constantly. We learned together, although I kept my distance from them, emotionally and even physically. I had been one to hug and touch, often, along with smiling, but now I kept a reserve around me.

During the early weeks, my nemesis in the classroom was Billy Ray. He vied for control of the classroom and his buddies followed him like the Pied Piper. Then one day after our morning kindergarten class was over, I saw Billy Ray being hauled down the hall by a big, scowling man. The boy was hitting about every third step of the man's.

I stopped both of them, using the chipper voice of the perennially cheerful kindergarten teacher. "You must be Billy Ray's father."

"No," the man replied, while Billy Ray cowered beside him. "But I'm as good as."

At that moment, there was nothing of the classroom mutiny leader about Billy Ray. I learned that day not to make assumptions, and not to forget that a five-year-old is still just a little child.

My normal inclination would have been to find an opportunity the next day to give Billy Ray a pat on the head, or a hug when he did "a good job." But while I empathized for him, I kept my physical and emotional detachment.

Then there was Odell. Two weeks into the school year, he told me at naptime that he wasn't going to lie down "for no honky." My teacher training fled, and the mother in me snapped back, "I don't care if I'm pink with blue polka dots, you're lying down on your nap rug." And he did.

I might have enjoyed the moment, even seen it as a hallmark of my control, but all my thoughts flowed back to Mikey, lying in the hospital.

It was October, and Mikey had been in the hospital for two weeks—an eternity. The children in my class had settled down some. We had reached an accord, it seemed. But I knew there was a distance between us. Truthfully, I felt awkward patting the children's plaited hair. The texture of their hair was so different from that of my own children's.

Then one day at naptime, I sat in a chair in the midst of the children who were lying on their nap rugs. As instructed in my teacher classes, I was modeling the behavior I wanted: be still and be quiet. My thoughts turned to Mikey, and I began to cry. Tears slipped down my cheeks and I brushed them away so the children wouldn't notice.

Then Billy Ray crept over and began patting me on my shoulder. Even Odell, his face concerned, came over. Another little one, Marikea, took hold of my hand. I drew her close, hugging her for comfort and kissed the top of her head. Deep within, I became keenly aware that this child—all the children—were bringing me solace of an honest kind.

Thirty-five years later, I often think of that day and of those children. They will always remain special and unforgettable to me.

They were a precious gift.

Coochie

By Brian Thornton

*I*t's COOCHIE!" the kilt-clad, spiky-haired freak shouted from the back of my new third-period English class. Titters followed close on the heels of his pronouncement.

It was my first day teaching this particular class. As expected, I was already getting an earful from one of the members of the class who was going to need particular attention.

"It says here that your name is 'Edward,'" I said.

"I don't go by that."

"I see. What should I call you, again?"

"Coochie" threw his head back and barked out his pre-ferred *nom-de-guerre* once again. Once again, his outburst brought giggles from many of the other kids in the room.

When I asked why he wished to be called "Coochie" (and I imitated his exaggerated manner of pronouncing his chosen moniker when I did so), he explained that it was his last name. I looked at the roster. His name read as "Edward Koedzhe." He then told me in no uncertain terms, that he did not like his first name, and never went by it.

"And you pronounce it 'coochie'?" I asked.

"Yes. Coochie's my name, and that's what I go by. I won't go by Edward. I don't like that name."

So I was faced by a pretty serious dilemma. On the one hand, knowing as I did the time-worn connotation of "coochie" as a rather unflattering reference to certain parts of female plumbing, I found the prospect of calling this kid "coochie" without bursting out laughing every time I spoke to him pretty daunting. On top of that, it was September, so I could anticipate having to refer to him in this manner for at least the next nine months.

On the other hand, if I didn't call him "coochie" every time I spoke to him, I could likely expect more grandstanding on his part. I made up my mind on the spot that I was going to have to take this a third way.

"Wow, cool name!" I said. "Do you have a sister?"

"Coochie" and the rest of the class seemed surprised by my question. "Yes," he said. "Two."

"What are their names?"

"Alicia and Stephanie."

"Nice names, but just think if your parents had been more imaginative, and called one or the other 'Hoochie.'" The other kids in class giggled. I'm pretty sure none of them had actually heard the term "hoochie coochie" before, but being thirteen-year-olds, and the phrase sounding nonsensical, they laughed. For his part, Edward Koedzhe's expression clouded at the mention of his parents. I made a note of that.

"So maybe, Mr. Koedzhe—" I began, careful to pronounce his last name the way he had, as "coochie."

"Not 'mister,'" he said, "Just 'Coochie.'"

"Well, you don't get to call me 'Brian,' any more than I get to call you 'Edward,' and since I consider calling me 'Thornton,' without the 'mister' in front of it to be disrespectful, it doesn't seem fair for me to do that to you. See what I'm saying?" He smiled for the first time, then said that he did. I continued.

"Imagine," I said to the class, "That Mr. Koedzhe grows up, graduates high school and college," more giggles at the mention of "college," ". . . and gets a good paying job, finds the right gal, gets married, and has a couple of kids.

"Now further imagine that he names her 'Hoochie.'" More laughter from the entire class, Edward Koedzhe included. "And once she in turn has grown up, gone to college, and found herself a good-paying job, she meets the guy of her dreams, and marries him, and let's say that his last name is 'Mann.'" They were following me pretty closely, waiting for me to put it all together, which I did.

"And since no child of Mr. Koedzhe would ever be anything other than her own person, she decides to hyphenate her maiden name and her married name. This would make her 'Hoochie Koedzhe-Mann.'"

They laughed again. One of the other kids in class, one who I found out later had a father who was a lover of blues music, spoke up and said, "Hey! Isn't that a song?"

I said it was. Kids laughed. Koedzhe laughed. We had a discussion about blues music, and how it helped give birth to rock, soul, funk, hip-hop, and so on.

Thus began my year-long association with Edward Koedzhe. I soon heard from other teachers that he could be disrespectful, that he was definitely a class clown, and that assessments of his academic ability ran the gamut from "he's a twisted, attention-loving genius" to "I think he might have autism."

My own take on him was that he was quite bright, but that he lacked motivation. When I spoke to our head counselor about him, she filled in some of the blanks for me. Edward's mother had a history of mental illness, including suffering from a form of bipolar disorder. She also had problems with alcohol. Edward was the eldest of three children, and he took extraordinary pride in caring for his two younger sisters. He made them breakfast and dinner, did their laundry, and most important got between them and their mother when she flew into one of her rages. Our head counselor had Child Protective Services on speed dial in large part because of Mr. Koedzhe.

On that first day, I got lucky with Edward Koedzhe. Because I was willing to meet him halfway on calling him by his last name, and on the pronunciation of said name (I soon learned that other teachers weren't), and apparently because of my explanation that calling him "mister" was a sign of respect, he never again gave me cause to wonder how I was going to "handle" him. This from a kid who wore T-shirts with the logo of the teen-angst-rock band "KORN" and wore kilts to school (I later discovered that the lead singer of this band wore kilts onstage, sort of like Axl Rose of Guns 'N Roses infamy). Mr. Koedzhe (and for me, he was always "Mr. Koedzhe") must have decided that I was alright, and he treated me accordingly.

The story doesn't end there, though. I kept hearing about this poor kid having trouble in other classes. Halfway through first quarter, our head counselor came to me and asked whether I'd like to have a student aide.

It turned out that Edward Koedzhe had gotten himself kicked out of one of his elective classes, and when he and the counselor were trying to work out a schedule change, he asked about being my student aide. I told her that in light of the circumstances, I didn't see how I could possibly refuse.

It was the best move I could have made. I've had a number of student aides over the years, but none worked as hard, or did more without being asked, than Edward Koedzhe did. In fact, on those rare occasions when I had to be out of the classroom, my substitute teachers all raved about what a terrific student aide I had, and how they wished they didn't have to wait until the end of the day to have him working for them. He even offered them assistance in his regular English class (since he now had me as his teacher twice per day).

Oh, and the kid aced English.

I lost track of Coochie once he moved on to bigger and better things (e.g., high school). I have no idea where he is now, or what he's doing, but I'm relatively certain that wherever it is, and whatever it is, he's doing it his way.

And good for him.

Sure Things

By Elizabeth Eidlitz

*D*uring graduation exercises, my mind often detours to those missing from pomp and circumstantial ranks—the expelled ones who refused to color between the lines, the boat rockers who insisted on learning in their own ways rather than waiting to be taught in ours.

I want to know that those challenging "rotten kids" who invite us to exchange energies, somewhere and somehow set records straight, survived, even triumphed. Like Nick Zachary.

I can still picture Nick orbiting seventh grade—a miniature Heathcliff with deep bruise-colored hair, a cynically curly mouth, and a stormy expression betrayed by eyes of Fra Angelico blue. The music teacher, who calls him impossible, begs me, as Dean of Students, to see for myself. Visiting her class, I maneuver to share Nick's copy of "The May

Day Carol." Not as precocious as those who crack up over the line "if not a bowl of your sweet cream . . ." Nick plays the disruptive game his own way.

"I have to go to the bathroom," he announces when the teacher acknowledges his raised hand.

Under her benign, "I think you can wait," he smells fear and wavering indecision.

"Want me to do it right here?"

The class suspends itself for her response. But only Nick speaks. He glances up at me to say, "She's handling me very badly, isn't she?"

How can I reprimand him while my guts are giggling?

The following year I walk out the side door of the school building just in time to see Nick bloody and break a classmate's nose. I grab Nick's arm as he prepares to deliver a knockout punch. Beyond the two boys, a squirrel lies by the foot of an oak, its tail swishing like a wild windshield wiper.

"Jay was stoning that squirrel to death!" Nick chokes back a sob, the first and last time I will see him near tears. "And I—I didn't think I'd hit him that hard."

It's the classic truth for eighth- and ninth-grade boys who haven't yet adjusted to new physical strength. When girls get angry, crumpled notebook paper misses the wastebasket; when boys get angry, fire doors fall, stained glass windows shatter, noses break.

By his freshman year, I meet Nick at eye level, unless he's hiding behind wraparound Ray-Bans that confront me with my own image. He combs his curly hair, now forsythia yellow, haphazardly, if at all.

The afternoon I proctor in the library where absolute silence rules, Nick taps a neighbor on the shoulder and whispers to him.

I intercept: "What are you doing, Nick?"

"I need a pencil. I was asking Daryl if I could borrow his."

"No," I say firmly.

"Yes," he frowns. "That is what I was doing."

Though still a bleached blond in tenth grade, Nick has traded curls for crew cut surfaces, engraved with skinhead Zs. Inked names of rock groups stripe one leg of jeans, ripped at the knees. Surprisingly, he picks up a piece of paper littering the corridor and drops it into the wastebasket, unaware that he's being noticed.

Detentions often keep him in late at school. Nick crosses the parking lot, hailing me with, "locked yourself out?" the afternoon I'm contemplating how to get at keys hanging from my VW's ignition.

"Yes."

"Wait a sec. I'll be right back."

He returns with a twisted coat hanger and—sure thing—puts me on the road within three minutes. He knew I'd look in my rear view mirror to see him grinning and waving as I leave.

We meet at the water cooler the next year.

"Gotta talk to you," he says. "Not here. Private. Your office?"

He follows me down the hall.

"You know Lisa," he begins.

I teach his girlfriend, a hardworking senior, not brilliant, but right-minded.

"Lisa just got turned down for Early Decision. I know her better than an Admissions Committee or even her teachers here. Skidmore made a mistake. So I found out our school code, pulled Lisa's folder from the secretary's files, and called the college's Head of Admissions. He's going to look into it and call me back."

"Call you back?"

"Sure thing. After they reconsider. They believe I'm the college counselor here. Yeah, I know I'll be caught. It had to be done and I wasn't scared when I did it. But now I am. I thought you'd understand."

"Have you told Lisa?"

"Negative. You gonna have to tell someone?"

"No, you are. But I'll go with you to the headmaster if you'd like."

He'd like. Since my business ends with moral support while Nick repeats the tale, I excuse myself. As I leave, Nick says, "Thanks, Liz."

Later we discuss formal conventions.

"No offense meant, Ms. Eidlitz. In there you just felt like my friend."

Second semester, my English elective class list includes "Zachary" for the first time. Nick slumps and yawns in the back row; his eyes often look bloodshot or glazed. He does little work. Nah—no need for a conference. "Just let me know when I'm going under D minus," he sneers.

Nick crams for the exam and gets through with a D plus, despite late and superficial papers. Outside of class I never see him. I suspect he avoids me. The faculty consider him "wasted," suspect drugs. All his grades have dropped by June. He's put on strict probation for senior year. One mistake—out.

The guidance counselor calls me during the summer. Will I take Nick on as an advisee? It's his request.

I agree on condition that he checks in with me daily.

"Not to infantilize you," I explain to Nick in September. "Just to take your emotional temperature."

His black T-shirt reads, "EAT RIGHT. KEEP FIT. DIE ANYWAY." He studies the leather watchband he wears with no timepiece in it and grins: "It's a deal."

"Nick, is there anyone in your class you really admire?"

"Sure thing," he answers promptly. "Neville Collias."

He's named a bland, laid-back C plus student. "Do you know why?"

"Yeah, but maybe I shouldn't say. Teachers don't always appreciate my word choice."

"Go ahead."

"Neville has his shit severely together."

It figures. Nick's shit always hits some fan.

"OK—here's the deal, Nick. You feel any desire to risk trouble, you find me first, even if the door's closed. I don't want to find out that you couldn't talk to me because I was teaching."

"Who else gets to interrupt your class like that?"

"No one. Why?"

"I'm not sure I want to be special."

"Everyone's special. Like everyone else, you get treated individually."

It works. Every day. Sometimes a wave from the hall, sometimes a circle formed by thumb and forefinger as he passes my doorway; sometimes drawings on my blackboard: A Kilroy figure labeled "Nick Was Here." A chalked monkey clinging to a banana peel: "Still hangin' in, Nick."

Some days he drops by in person, though not to talk: he's sorry, has to run—a class, sports, his job at McDonald's. But he looks turned up 200 watts.

The day he stays long enough to show me something he treasures more than anything in the world, he pulls a red plastic disk from the shirt pocket that buttons over his heart: his 90-day token from Alcoholics Anonymous.

Then one November morning as I stand by the window, teaching a class, I see Nick flipping side view mirrors of faculty cars parked on the exit road as he walks off campus, cuts between rows of tombstones in the adjacent cemetery, and vanishes.

He's waiting in my classroom after lunch.

"They bagged me."

I sit beside him. "What made you leave?"

"Needed a physics book."

"Couldn't have borrowed one?"

"Not one with my notes in it."

Too quick, too slick, too Nick. But the lie isn't the issue.

He sighs and says, "I'll get busted, right?"

"Probably." Giving him another chance after the last chance would persuade him of what he already suspects: people rarely mean what they say.

"You can't—don't you want to save me?"

"I think you're testing the school. Asking us to expel you. What you'll do next with a fresh start? Any ideas?"

His fingers drum the chair arm. "Not a clue. Gotta go, clean out my desk, my locker . . ." He's started for the doorway when I say, "Hey, Nick—You don't have to be enrolled here for me to care about you. Couldn't I stop by at McDonald's for a hamburger with you someday?"

"Sure thing." It's a scornful tone, flattened by disenchantment. I've failed him.

No one hears from or about Nick. It seems intrusive to turn into the golden arches on my way home.

I'm discussing fate, chance, and coincidence with a last period class three years later when a clear-skinned young man in an army uniform opens my classroom door. In front of fourteen stunned ninth graders Nick comes toward my desk, kisses me on the cheek, and whispers, "Finally got my shit severely together. Can we get that hamburger now?"

"After class. In ten minutes."

He steers for an empty seat. I ask for volunteers to read parts in *Oedipus Rex*. Nick raises his hand for Tiresias.

While his rare hamburger drips, he tells me he likes army structure, the discipline, the fact that every individual belongs to a group. But he's getting out, planning to go to college, eventually work with animals. Greenpeace maybe. He wants to save whales, children, the planet.

"My treat," he says, opening his wallet. Among dollar bills he still keeps a photograph of Japanese cranes he clipped from a library copy of *National Geographic*.

"Did you know my parents split?"

I shake my head. I'd never met the Zacharys. Not even on Parents' Night.

"Yeah. Well they did. My dad's moved to Provincetown. Living with another guy. The day I got busted I'd just found out. I felt everyone at school looking at me funny, like it was written all over my knees and elbows that my father was gay. Had to get outta here, get away."

"Stay in touch, please," I tell him in the parking lot as we head in different directions. Nicks spins off into five years of darkness. Then one April day, having found my home address, he turns his motorcycle into my driveway. His hair, yellow again, ends in a comet's tail. The girl clutching his waist, looking at him adoringly, wears a bedspread dress and Birkenstocks. He introduces her by the name she's just taken legally: "Jonatha Ariadne Caspian." Both go to UNH. Spring break now. Just thought he'd stop by to check in. Couple of minutes for a Coke? Sure thing. Then they vroom-vroom off into another space.

It's years before the next sighting. Returning from school one spring afternoon, I see the L.L.Bean label on Nick's jeans as he bends over my tulips to weed them. His head comes up with natural brown curls under the control of expert scissors. At thirty, Nick has started to find himself—severely.

He's off to the West Coast in a week to lead rafting expeditions. Jonatha? She's history. "While I was crying in my guts over a newspaper photo of an oil-slicked bird in the Gulf, she was laughing at the comics. It wasn't going to work."

Some heavenly bodies rotate in regular fashion; comets never follow rules. Nick moves in a highly elongated ellipse. I can't predict the date of his next return from an uncharted course, only another confluence of our lives one of these surprising years.

Nick taught me that there's no such thing as a "rotten kid." Scratch any outrageous behavior and you'll glimpse the cause of it. It matters to me that Nick still wants to swing by so that I can see for myself that he's okay. And it matters to Nick that it still matters to me.

Sure thing.

A Dream Fulfilled

By Kyle Richtig

I became a teacher to help people learn. I did not know that when I became a teacher I would be helping people fulfill their dreams.

My classroom does not cater to those in school in the traditional sense. My students are those who have entered the workforce, been injured in the workplace, and are trying to enhance their skills so that they can return to the workforce. One of these students was Lisa.

Lisa came to me in her forties. She had two children in high school, and had returned to work because she had left her husband due to his substance abuse. She worked hard to earn money to keep her children's lives stable, which was difficult, as she did not have a high school diploma.

Lisa was in high school in the 1970s, wherein someone could leave school midway through high school and still get a job. When she re-entered the workforce in the 1990s, the educational requirements for individuals had changed. Lisa was able to secure a job, which required a great deal of physical strength, moving bags of chocolate in a chocolate factory. Moving the bags over the years strained her muscles and damaged her arm to the point where surgery could only restore seventy percent of the mobility.

Because Lisa's injury was at work, she was eligible for help re-entering the workforce. When I started with Lisa, she had a great deal of difficulty with her work. She had not been in school for twenty-five years, and had not used many of her skills in quite a long time. We worked on a plan to get Lisa in a position to go to college as a mature student. She was pleased with her program, but had always wanted to receive her high school diploma.

Lisa and I decided that along with her studies to prepare for college, we were going to work towards her obtaining her GED. Because of her drive, Lisa was able to carry on both programs. We had no difficulties until Lisa went to visit her doctor. She told Lisa that she was going to require another surgery to correct the injuries in her arm. Lisa's surgery was scheduled for two months later, and we had to finish all of her studies before the surgery. The recovery time from the surgery, as well as the physiotherapy, would use up all of the remaining time before she would start her college programs.

We worked fast to finish her requirements, and Lisa and I set a date for her to take her GED exams. I ran pre-GED tests and Lisa passed all of the subjects with higher grades than necessary to receive her GED.

The GED examinations were not available in our city, so Lisa had to travel a few hours away to take the tests. She spent two days in testing, and when she arrived back to school, we waited anxiously for the results.

Lisa brought the results in from her GED testing a week later. She handed me the opened envelope without telling me verbally, or through her body the results. I opened the envelope cautiously, and read the results.

I think that I was more disappointed than Lisa. She had passed five of the six subject areas, and the one that she didn't pass, she had only missed by a few marks.

❄ ❄ ❄ ❄

"I can't believe that they didn't pass you because of a few marks." I was angry because we had worked so hard, and because it was unfair that she had to travel to another city to take the test, so that someone who lived locally would have been fresher for it after waking up in their own bed.

"To be honest, I am happy that I was able to do this well. Before I came here, I didn't have the confidence to take this test. It's taken twenty years, and you telling me that I am capable to get this far."

I took a great deal of joy from Lisa's triumph, but was not about to allow her to fail at something she had worked so hard for. I found out that Lisa had to wait before she could take the test again, but because she had passed all areas but the math portion, she would only need to retake the math test. Unfortunately, the next test she was eligible to take wasn't until after her surgery.

Lisa and I only had a few weeks left together after she received the results of her GED test. We focused the rest of our time on solidifying Lisa's math skills, and scheduled her next GED math test for after her surgery. She left for her surgery, and we lost touch.

Months passed, and I thought of Lisa and hoped that her surgery went well. I knew that surgery was not pleasant for anyone, and that the rehabilitation may have overshadowed Lisa's plans to take her GED math examination. Even if Lisa had taken the test, it would have been months after she had last worked on the math program.

One day I was teaching my new students, and Lisa showed up. She came into my class with a huge smile on her face. She handed me an envelope, which contained her GED diploma.

"You did it!" I said jumping up from my chair.

"I owe this all to you," Lisa said giving me a hug. "It goes to show you can teach an old dog new tricks."

Lisa, armed with her GED, started college and continues to pursue her dream of becoming a social worker. I learned that no one's dreams are unattainable, and that there is no greater joy than helping others reach for the stars.

Embarrassment

By Anna Cody

*L*unchtime was over for the third grade, and the spotlight was on our "Student of the Week." Jeri was standing in front of her classmates, displaying a prized soccer trophy and fielding questions from the other students about her athletic accomplishments. Instead of offering Jeri the full attention she deserved during this special time, I had momentarily turned my back to return a few files to the cabinet behind my desk.

Suddenly I heard a giggle, then a gasp.

"Mrs. Cody," a boy said. "Jeri went to the bathroom."

I turned toward the students.

"On the floor!" someone added.

Oh, no. There stood Jeri in the front of the room, legs crossed. At her feet was a little yellow puddle.

Immediately I had visions of Jeri's dismal future—taunts on the playground, nicknames at the bus stop. Years from now, children from Room 26 might remember Jeri only as "that girl who wet her pants in front of the whole class."

I knew I had two options:

1. Draw as little attention as possible to the incident by casually wiping up the puddle myself while instructing the students to open their social studies books and begin reading the section on Thomas Jefferson and the Louisiana Purchase; or

2. Call a custodian to clean up the mess while conducting an informal class discussion about how embarrassing incidents happen to us all, and we wouldn't want anybody to tease us if we had wet our pants, now would we?

I decided on a combination of the two. Jeri left for the nurse's office where she could call home for a dry change of clothes, and I matter-of-factly cleaned up the floor with antiseptic wipes while engaging the children in a conversation about how uncomfortable Jeri probably felt right now. We were all sure that she felt pretty bad, and we agreed it would be best if nobody mentioned this little "accident" ever again. Still, I was skeptical. These were eight-year-olds, after all. The temptation to tell other playground chums about the excitement during our "Student of the Week" time might be too great.

But the rest of the day passed without incident, and the next and the next. Nobody reported any teasing, and Jeri showed up every morning with a smile on her face and went home with the smile still in place. Clearly, I'd worried over nothing.

A couple of weeks passed before I realized my little "talk" about embarrassing incidents may have had more of an impact than I originally thought.

It was Friday morning, and I was giving the weekly spelling test. I wandered between the rows of desks while pronouncing each spelling word. I had just passed Troy's desk when I heard him whisper loudly to me, "Mrs. Cody, you have a hole in your pants."

Startled, I looked down at the legs of my dark-colored slacks. The little girl sitting next to Troy leaned over to help. "It's in the back."

I ran my left hand up and down the back of my slacks. The material had grown thin and had separated in a long vertical tear right next to the back pocket, exposing what I imagined to be an expanse of gleaming white underwear.

I backed toward the classroom door, hoping to flag down somebody to watch over my class while I figured out the quickest way to mend my pants or find another pair. My face must have looked an awful lot like Jeri's had a few weeks before.

As I eased past the last row of desks near the door, Brad looked up at me earnestly. In his most consoling voice, likely gleaned from listening to his mother soothe some past slight or humiliation, he whispered, "Don't worry, Mrs. Cody. We didn't really see much."

Thank goodness.

I was relatively sure my little secret would stay safely within the confines of our classroom walls, instead of becoming fodder for lunch table humor. These kids really understood about embarrassment.

Still, I'm enough of a realist to know that someday, someone will remind Jeri that she wet her pants in front of the whole class in third grade. And somebody else will say, "Yeah, and remember during the spelling test when we saw the teacher's underwear?"

Just hopefully not too soon.

Why I Did It

By Julie T. Anderson

What the hell am I doing here? When I entered the classroom on the first day of school, seventeen absurdly young faces looked up at me and my breath became fast and shallow. I wondered if my expression betrayed my shock. As I scanned the room; my students were ninth graders but many of them—especially the boys—were so small, they looked like they couldn't possibly be any older than eight or nine. A kid called Ben, whose head barely reached the top of the table, cracked his gum, poked the girl sitting next to him, then gave me a big, devilish smile. *Crap,* I thought, this is *definitely* a bad idea.

People often ask me why I did it. Why give up two tenure-track job offers at universities to teach English at a high school? The fact of the matter is, those first few months I asked myself the same question. While teaching my ninth-grade classes, all I could think of was how quiet and orderly my university students had been, how nicely they sat in their chairs, how well they listened to instructions.

By contrast, this group of ninth graders, whom I taught at the end of the day, could barely sit still for five minutes. Many of the boys seemed to me to have some sort of physical impairment because they kept shifting and moving in their seats, dropping their books, standing up inexplicably in the middle of class to saunter over to the pencil sharpener or trash bin. The girls, in turn, were easily distracted by the boys and would whisper incessantly to their classmates. I was appalled to learn I had to separate kids—it seemed so juvenile to me. Why wouldn't they just sit still and behave? And why couldn't I just have a *conversation* with them about the reading, rather than having to switch from one activity to another to accommodate their frustratingly short attention spans? While teaching that ninth-grade classic, *The Catcher in the Rye,* I was keenly in touch with Holden's depression. Like him, I felt there was something terribly wrong with the world but, at the same time, I was also aware that I had consciously, almost purposefully, screwed up my own life.

I hadn't realized until I left academia how much I liked, indeed, relied upon the status the university had accorded me. At parties, when people asked me what I did, I would modestly reply that I was studying for a Ph.D. in Comparative Literature, specializing in Ancient Greek, Roman, and Chinese poetry. "Wow," they would say, "can you actually *understand* all those languages?" "Why, yes," I'd answer, secretly enjoying their astonishment and admiration. "No big deal."

Now, when I explained to people that I taught high school, they would nod their heads politely then drift away. This loss of status, combined with the unpredictable energy and short attention spans of my new students, left me overwhelmed and confused. Some days during that semester, I thought I might simply stay in bed and refuse to go to work. I even contemplated asking one of the colleges for the job I had so brashly turned down. I got as far as dialing the number once or twice and hearing the phone ring before hanging up.

That was what was so odd. I *could* have called and asked for the position because the college hadn't filled it. And yet, I was never able to go through with the call. I had left academia for a reason—I wanted to teach, not to research, I wanted the daily intimacy with students that occurs at a high school, not a college—and some small part of me still remembered this.

I'd like to say there was one transcendent moment when I realized that I had made the right choice to teach high school. It happened as a series of smaller moments, each one easing my sense of loss, replacing it with a glimpse of joy, till one day I realized my grief had lifted, rather like a balloon on a string that quietly floats off without your noticing.

The first of the little moments that led to this lifting happened when I mentioned to my students that I lived in China for two years. They got all quiet, shushing each other, then asked me with bated breath if I would tell them a story about my life there. Or, another time, when I consented to have class outside, the kids clapped their hands with such unbridled joy I couldn't help but get a bit giddy myself. And then there was the time when they performed five-minute renditions of the *Odyssey;* their enthusiasm and silliness made the skits wonderful—far better than anything my college students, mindful of their dignity, could have done.

Particular students come to mind, too. One day I asked Alec, a very sweet and earnest child, if he'd "like to answer" a question. He looked at me very seriously and said, "No thanks, I wouldn't like to answer it right now." His response was so ingenuous that the whole class burst into laughter. He looked around, pleased but confused. "Alec, *would* you answer this question?" I said, rephrasing my request. "Oh yes," he replied, "certainly." Another student, Gabe, asked me one day if I would address him that afternoon as Melvin Rabinowitz. When I asked him why, he raised his hands in the air, shrugged, and said, "'Cause I just feel like it."

One of my very favorite moments came in early June. Throughout the year, I used to tell my students, as I handed back papers, that their grades weren't a reflection of who they were as people or of what I thought of them. When I passed out student evaluations in June, the students could see I was quite nervous. "Now, now," Carolyn said, wagging a finger at me, barely able to contain her smile, "don't be nervous. These evaluations aren't a reflection of who you are as a person or of what we think of you, you know!"

Reading through the evaluations later, I was moved at how appreciative the students had been of my efforts and how sweetly candid they were. One child wrote about me, "She is lots of fun and English is one of my favorite classes so please don't fire her!" Another called my comments on her writing "PRICELESS." It felt good, too, to see the considerable changes in my ninth graders' writing and analytical skills that had occurred by the end of the year; these changes were far greater than any I had witnessed in a college student. What's more, the evaluations expressed real affection for me—love, actually—that surprised and moved me.

A few days after the evaluations, a friend from London came for a visit. When I started telling him about my job—about the ninth-grade students and all the funny, wonderful things they did—Giles stirred his coffee for a moment then looked up at me and said, "You know, I think you actually *like* your job. No. I take it back, I think you *love* it."

It dawned on me then that he was right. When I consider what I gave up—prestige, a lot of time spent immersed in books and papers in small, lonely rooms, students who sit still but don't clap their hands or beg you to tell them a story—it seems a small price to pay for the joy I get from teaching high school.

I now know why I did it.

Saving a Life

By Anne Forbes as told by John Young

*M*y father, Ted Forbes, was a teacher most of his life. The last school he taught in was Gompers Jr. High School in Joliet, Illinois, near Chicago. The kids were tough but the teachers were tougher. Long before there was Columbine, one student at Gompers was out shooting at cars with a rifle. The principal snuck up on him from behind and grabbed the kid. We never heard about it on the news.

Yet, there are teachers who make a difference. My father believed that all students could do well. He would work with students and often succeeded in helping them, in spite of themselves. We never knew anything about it because Dad was modest, even though his was a forceful personality. Here is one student's success we heard about from my cousin, Johnny Young.

❄ ❄ ❄ ❄

My plane was still boarding. As Vice President for a Missouri insurance company, I traveled extensively and was now headed from Oklahoma City to Chicago. Almost everyone had boarded. A young black man entered the plane. The kid was twenty-something, dressed in jeans and a shirt, carrying a big stack of big books. I guessed he was a college student. The plane was virtually full. The only seats left were in the center.

At that time, passengers were not assigned specific seats. In this plane, there were three seats on the left and three on the right. What usually happened was that one person took the window seat and one took the aisle seat. Then they piled stuff in the middle, coats, pillows, anything to make the center seat off-limits.

As the young black man continued walking down the long aisle, I observed that no one offered him the center seat. As he approached, instead of trying to shield my center seat, I gave him a friendly "Hello," knowing he would sit in the seat beside me. And he did. The young man was nice looking, a sharp guy. His speech was excellent and he was interested in talking. I asked him if he was a student. He said he was at the University of Oklahoma at Norman, Oklahoma, majoring in engineering. I knew he was no dummy because you have to be sharp to graduate from any engineering school anywhere. He was in the upper ranks at school and a senior about ready to graduate.

He said he was from Chicago.

"How did you happen to get into school way down in Oklahoma? You must have been making awfully good grades to get into engineering school."

He stared at me. "You won't believe the story of my life."

I encouraged him to elaborate.

When he was in junior high school, his mother worked in his school cafeteria and that embarrassed him. He didn't know who his dad was, which embarrassed him, too. He described the terrible social situation in which he found himself. "At that point of my life, I was just a N-----. I carried a brickbat. I was a screw-up. I carried the brickbat because I was a rotten student and did rotten things."

"What's a brickbat?" I asked.

"A brickbat is a small piece of brick you hold in your hand." He demonstrated with an imaginary brick. "I could break your arm."

I must have looked shocked because he shook his head in disgust at his former self.

"I made terrible grades and only went to class when I had to," he said, sadly. "All I wanted to do was lash out at the world." He continued for some minutes describing his former self in the most derogatory terms. "In that early part of my life, I had no pride in myself. I was a no-good kid with no ambition." He lowered his head thinking about his former actions. "I felt I was the lowest form of animal."

"One day," he took a breath and straightened up, "one of my teachers told me I had as good a brain and as good a mind as anybody in the school and that I could do anything I wanted to do and that I was using my social position to goof off and not do well."

"Naturally, I didn't belive him." He eyed me. "Why would a white teacher want to help a black student?"

"I hope that every teacher, black or white, would want to help every student," I said sincerely.

The young man stared at me. Clearly, his experience had been different. "This teacher was special," he countered. "Every time I got in trouble, this teacher found out about it. He told me, 'See, you're doing just what I said you'd do'." The young man raised a finger and shook it at me as if I were him getting lectured by the teacher. "If you keep messing up, you could go to jail and stay in the gutter, *or* you can be one of the best students in this school."

I smiled at his rendition.

"Can you believe that this was my science teacher?" he asked me.

I shook my head, but then thought to myself that my cousin, Ted, taught science.

The young man looked at me earnestly. "This teacher kept telling me I had the brains to do whatever I wanted to do. He told me it was that simple. I could use my social background as an excuse *or* I could use my brain. He kept after me and after me."

The young man waved his hand in the air as if waving away his former self. "After awhile, I decided to do some homework to show this teacher that I couldn't make it in school." He looked at me. "Nobody was as surprised as I was when I found I *could* do the work. The teacher made me stay after school and work because I had a lot of catching up to get even with the other junior high school kids. I started looking up to the teacher and doing what the teacher said."

The young man smiled. "By this time, my mother thought the science teacher was the most wonderful guy on earth."

"After that, it was simple. Once I learned how to study, I went through high school making good grades. I don't mean I didn't have to work at it, but now I knew I could do it. I didn't have a chip on my shoulder anymore. I had pride in myself." His face radiated confidence. "I could do anything I wanted—even become an engineer." The young man finished his incredible story with, "I owe my life to that man."

An idea popped in my head. I was going to take a wild guess. "You are describing a teacher I know," I said. "I bet I can tell you the name of that teacher."

We locked eyes.

"Ted Forbes," I announced.

I'll never forget the look of surprise on his face. His eyes grew as big as his books. Mine must have, too. He was as shocked as I was that I got it right. Here were two strangers from different states on an airplane with one person in common in Joliet, Illinois.

"How could you possibly know that?" The young man's voice was full of amazement.

"My guess was based on several clues from your story— junior high school, science teacher, white man, and it just sounded just like Ted. He's my cousin." I was grinning. "My biggest leap was guessing that you are from the Chicago area, not Chicago itself."

"Yes, I'm from Joliet," he confirmed.

The rest of the trip we talked about our experiences with Ted and how amazing this coincidence was but what was more amazing was that Ted was quietly helping students to save their lives.

❊ ❊ ❊ ❊

My father gave us three months to say goodbye. While he was in the hospital those three months, many of his former students stopped by to say how much he had helped them and thanked him for believing in them.

At Dad's funeral, many former students came to pay their respects. Two sisters, both former students, sang at Dad's funeral. One of the sisters, Mary Opal, saved her sister from drowning by using information that Dad gave her in school, but that's another story. We're just grateful that Dad knew how to give of himself. Many lives are touched by good teachers. My father was one of the best.

Anne

Giving Birth

By Sarah Raymond

ammy sat cross-legged in front of her locker. She was lost in her knitting needles, clicking out a white panel, as though knitting were as natural as finishing math homework. I was on hall duty.

I taught art to Tammy and her boyfriend Jeff. They were students who reminded me of certain couples from my own teenage years—the ones always side-by-side in the halls, so used to each other's company that they would run out of things to say. The as-good-as-married couples with the promise rings.

When Tammy's wardrobe started to change, I suspected she was pregnant. Instead of jeans, she began wearing outdated stretch pants, which were eventually overhung by a belly that grew robust and round and was tented by Jeff's hockey shirt. Jeff held his place next to Tammy in the halls.

As her belly surged outward, teachers in the staffroom raised questions about the couple's future. Everyone recognized that Tammy was too far along to think about an abortion. A younger teacher began a tenor rendition of "Here Comes the Bride." Another remembered her own era, when a pregnant teenager politely left her hometown for the duration of her pregnancy, and a sympathetic relative suddenly gained a new offspring.

As Tammy's belly swelled, her mascara disappeared. She seemed to turn inward, curling into herself with her fetus, and she sent out a silent message that she wasn't interested in talking about her situation. Her absences multiplied later in her pregnancy, and during one of them, Jeff mentioned to me after class the possibility of giving the baby up for adoption.

Both Tammy and Jeff were steady students. They were the reliable ones, who got their projects in on time. Neither had plans for leaving their small Ontario town. Tammy, who might have been pretty behind her straight brown hair, often stood behind Jeff, who was a broad, waddling sort of boy with an open smile. But she was alone knitting when I saw her in front of the locker that day, just after the fall term had begun.

Tammy was knitting yarn of a softness and fineness reserved for baby clothes. Her belly had returned, almost, to its regular seventeen-year-old proportions. The sight of her knitting convinced me that Tammy's plans for adoption had changed. I imagined she had fallen in love with the being she gave birth to, and couldn't bring herself to hand her most awesome creation to another woman's arms. I could understand the depth of such a loss. My husband and I were trying to get pregnant that year, and I'd already formed a surprising attachment to my own unfertilized eggs. Maybe Tammy's mother was helping to raise the child or maybe she and Jeff had found an apartment above a store on Main Street.

I stopped to talk to Tammy, knitting at her locker. Ever the art teacher, I asked about her handiwork. Tammy, previously our quiet, let's-not-discuss-this-enormous-belly-of-mine Tammy, began to talk. She told me she gave birth to a baby girl in the summer. Tammy held up her white panel to show me the fine stitches, and she dug through her backpack to find the other parts of the sweater. And then Tammy told me her plans for mailing the sweater to Kitchener, Ontario—to the couple who had adopted her baby. The new mother, Beth, couldn't have children. She and her husband were both lawyers, Tammy told me, with a hint of pride in her baby's new lineage. She and Beth had named the baby girl together.

As Tammy described her relationship with her baby's mother, her voice clear and strong, I was struck by Tammy's belief in the rightness of her decision, and her acceptance of giving away her baby to new parents who were in a better place in their lives for childrearing. The bell rang, and Jeff arrived at her locker. I hugged him. Tammy showed me another ball of yarn still wrapped in its label—a bigger, brighter ball. She was already thinking about the next, slightly larger sweater.

Mr. Never Give Up

By Carol Zook

*I*t didn't take long to realize that David was special in many ways. He bounded into my kindergarten classroom full of energy, talking loudly, and walking with a clumsy gait. From the first day, I knew David would need special attention.

In the first few weeks of school, David had problems with tasks the other students found fun. "Keep trying," I'd urge as he struggled to control his scissors during art. Writing his name was nearly impossible. "Let me help, David," I'd say. His hand shook so much that when I covered it with mine to help him write, my hand trembled also.

Our theme in kindergarten that year dealt with children's authors. David's favorite was H. A. Rey who wrote *Curious George*. While David had trouble with motor activities, he loved story time, and enjoyed our "Author of the Month" theme. He contributed freely to our discussions about books.

At conference time, I suggested that his parents take David to their doctor for an evaluation. They did and informed me that David had been diagnosed with hydrocephalus. Although his head wasn't as large as most patients with this affliction, he had extra fluid in his cranium. He was scheduled for surgery to insert a shunt that would relieve the pressure in his head and drain the excess fluid. This shunt would need to be replaced several times as he grew.

On the day after the surgery, when I was to go to the hospital to visit him, our monthly book order arrived. I gathered David's books to take with the cards the children had made him and the gift I had gotten.

My first thought as I entered the room was that David looked so fragile. His therapist was in the room working with him on walking. These first attempts after the surgery were shaky and halting. Seeing David drag his leg was hard to watch. During the therapy session, David's mother and I talked. "The doctor said that the fluid squirted all over him when they implanted the shunt," she said with tears in her eyes.

After the session, I gave David what I had brought. He loved his classmates' cards and enjoyed my stuffed toy, but the books were his favorite. "My books," he yelled. He had his mom read one book. Then I read another. He impressed his mom when he told her some of the things he had learned about H. A. Rey. "He carried the *Curious George* story on his bike when he was running away from the bad guys," he said. It was a wonderful visit. I held my tears until I got to my car, and didn't leave the parking garage for some time.

David improved quickly and was soon back in the classroom. I worried about the other children playing too roughly with him because he had been an active boy. I was also concerned that one of the children would say something unkind because he was wearing a dressing that covered the side of his head. My concerns were unfounded, however, because the children were gentle and kind. His return to the classroom went more smoothly that I had hoped.

It was my pleasure to see David grow up. He returned to our elementary school several times to visit. He didn't lose his freckles and his reddish-brown hair. The loud voice and big grin still remain. School was always difficult for David, but he worked hard and didn't give up. Graduation day was very special. After struggling in high school, everyone was happy to see that he had earned his diploma. Walking across the stage, he had a huge smile. His parents beamed. It took David a year longer to reach his goal of graduation, but that made the achievement sweeter.

I am thrilled to see the man he has become. David has worked very hard and has overcome many of the difficulties he has faced. "Mr. Never Give Up" has a job, is proud of his car, and enjoys life. He has achieved what I wish for all of my students—contentment with who he is.

Modern Magic

By Marcia Gabet

*T*here is much discussion today about dealing with diversity in America's schools. For generations of American history, public school classrooms have been the site of a miraculous blending of people of all nations and races. Today, the school classroom remains a common ground for the meeting of these cultures. The classroom is often where children learn acceptance and respect for people of different backgrounds. For thirty years, I had the unique opportunity of working with a remarkable culture, the Amish.

Amish children rewarded me with a variety of learning experiences in teaching in my rural northeastern Indiana community. The one-room Amish schools in our district begin with first grade, so my public school kindergarten classroom was usually comprised of two-thirds "English" students (as some of the Amish community thought of any non-Amish) and one-third Amish children. After their kindergarten year, most of the children would leave our public school and go on to first grade at an Amish school.

In today's schools we use "English as a Second Language" to help reach Hispanic and other non-English-speaking students. There was no help of that kind in my rural classroom. Many of my Amish students spoke German and little or no English at the beginning of the school year. Because the dialect was geared toward their own community, it was difficult to communicate in their language. So they came to my classroom shyly and voicelessly, through a strong desire on the part of their parents that they get off to a good start in school, and also to learn the English language.

These children were wide-eyed with the wonder of things they had never experienced or even understood. So they became adept at watching other students who were following my directions and they patterned that behavior. Amish parents recognized the beginning of their child's school career was also the time to learn the English language, so at that point in their young lives, the children received a double dose of English, both at home and in school. They usually picked up on the language enough to get along successfully in kindergarten.

I enjoyed the innocence and eagerness of the Amish children but I also greatly appreciated their parents. If a report card or a conference showed their child to be deficient in any skill, within a week or two, the child would have mastered that skill because the parents worked with them diligently until they showed some success at it. A high value was placed on their child's early education, possibly because all schooling finished at the end of eighth grade. At that time in their lives, they were expected to help with chores at home until they were old enough to be hired for a job of manual labor. The girls were not exempt from outside jobs until they were married and had children. They saved their earned income for a future marriage. Their income also helped to stock their "hope chest" which had begun filling with very early birthdays. It was not unusual for a five-year-old girl to receive a gift of a pretty dish for her hope chest. Our Show and Tell times also divulged that toy horses and tools were the most common gifts for young boys. One of their favorite tool items was a homemade nail bag or belt. The girls loved dolls and I was always amused to see them bring Barbies to Show and Tell, often in traditional Amish clothing.

The Amish parents showed gratitude for their children's schooling by sending me gifts of homemade baked goods, fruits and vegetables, jams and jellies, flowers and flower seeds, a plucked chicken or even fresh sausage from a hog slaughtered just that morning. Their appreciation was demonstrated in ways used for hundreds of years; they gave gifts made or grown with their own hands.

The children loved all things modern but they often needed instruction on the use of items common to the rest of us. Once, soon after a school year began, I discovered (through a sharp ammonia smell in our classroom) a boy was using the floor drain in the restroom for urinating. The lesson on toilet use and flushing, with no demonstration and given in an unrecognizable language, had apparently been beyond his understanding! The Amish children loved getting cool drinks from the water fountains with a touch of their fingertips and they loved the running water in the bathroom sink which was at just the right height for five- and six-year-olds. The liquid soap dispenser was the source of so many giggles and bubbles, I often had to remind them not to play in the sink. Even the use of the paper towel dispenser needed a demonstration or I would find yards of towels in the trash cans or toilets. Of course, the school bus ride was a favorite for everyone.

Videos were also a favorite, whether it was fiction or nonfiction. In my earlier days of teaching, everything was shown on 16-millimeter film, using a projector which cast the images on a screen. One of my most memorable moments of teaching was of one small, blonde-headed Amish boy named Lester.

I had shown a 16-millimeter film to the class but because the room had received a recent summer painting, the pull-down projection screen had not been reinstalled. So I substituted something else. I showed the film on a blank wall. The next day I received this note from Lester's mother:

Dear Mrs. Gabet,

Lester was so excited when he came home yesterday. He said he saw moving pictures with talking people on the wall in your room. He looked all around the wall where the pictures were moving but didn't see cords or plugs or anything which used electricity. He's convinced you have a magic wall! Oh, the innocence of children!

Sincerely,
Mrs. Irmsher

Lester's wonderment at my "magic" wall is something I will never forget. That same sense of the excitement of discovery was shared by students of all backgrounds as they entered our school. The classroom will forever remain a place where children gain not only knowledge, but an appreciation of different cultures and the ability to live and prosper as part of the miracle of the Great American Melting Pot.

Star Student

By Kathleen Reif-Burke

I was handing out the final exam when I heard a knock on my classroom door, not loud, but urgent. Like a phone call in the middle of the night, it was a dark disruption, filling my head with visions of car wrecks and broken legs. A late student wouldn't have knocked. Had my daughter been hurt? Papers in hand, I cracked the door open to find a sobbing coed.

Handing the final essay topics to a student to distribute, I walked into the hall of Old Main while the girl dug at her eyes with a knot of tissue.

"Are you Ms. Reif?"

"Yes."

"Kyle asked me to come tell you he won't be able to take the final."

Again, dire thoughts whirled through my mind. The situation had to be dire, because Kyle was my star student. He had an "A" going into the final. He was a talented writer with much to say, not about the topics that usually occupy freshmen writers, what's it like to live at the dorm or getting through rush week, but about social issues and current events. In a writing class, finding a Kyle was like discovering a nugget of gold in a pile of rocks. He always jumped to my bait—the interactive questions that got students thinking.

"What happened?" I asked, hearing my voice crack.

"He just can't take the final." The girl seemed ready to burst into a new round of tears as she turned to run down the hall.

"Wait," I called out. "Can't you tell me what's wrong?"

"He . . . he likes you," she said over her shoulder. "And asked me to come tell you. That's all."

"Tell me what?"

But she was gone. I heard her boots clatter as she ran down the curving staircase in the old campus building.

❊ ❊ ❊ ❊

That night after grading the final in-class essays, I stared at the fatal empty square where Kyle's final grade should have been. Technically, I was supposed to flunk him. But how could I flunk my star student? I got my file cards out and did something that writing teachers rarely do—looked up his home number and called him.

He answered on the first ring.

"Mr. Adams, this is Ms. Reif, your English Comp teacher."

A pause. "Oh yeah, Ms. Reif. Hi. Didn't Carly come by?"

"Yes, your friend came and told me you couldn't take the final. But she didn't say why. If you don't take the final, you flunk. I don't want to flunk you, Mr. Adams. You're my star student."

He laughed a little, sniffed a little. "I'm a star?"

"Best writer in the class."

"You always argue with me."

"I'm trying to get you to think, that's all. It's nothing personal."

"Everything," he said. "Everything is personal."

"What's wrong, Mr. Adams? Have I offended you in some way?"

"Lots of times," he said. "All the times you asked the class to divide by gender and discuss male/female issues, feminism, equal pay, all that."

"Critical thinking technique, Mr. Adams. It gets the class off dorm topics."

Again, a little laugh. "There are other gender options, Ms. Reif."

It hit me then, and even as the truth sunk home, I thought Kyle didn't fit the stereotype. He didn't look gay—a muscular, ruggedly handsome kid with a crooked, engaging grin. He looked like a football player. So much for my sensitivity and critical thinking skills.

I sat down at my desk, hands shaking. "I'm sorry, Mr. Adams. I guess I teach with heterosexuality in mind. It wasn't very sensitive."

"It's not your fault," he said. "Everything's like that. There's no place to fit in."

I didn't like the uncharacteristic defeatist tone. "Finals aren't over yet," I said. "Why don't you come in tomorrow? Write one fifty-minute essay. No big deal, not for you."

"Can't," he mumbled.

"Why not?"

It came tumbling out then. "I've had a partner for almost a year. He's a law student. Yesterday, he told me he tested positive for AIDS. I'm leaving school. It seems pointless now."

My throat constricted, and I grabbed the cold cup of coffee on my desk and gulped it. "Do your parents know?"

"They don't even know I'm gay." Tinged with the kind of savage bitterness felt only by the hopeless young. I thought of all the suicide studies on late adolescence.

"Where will you go?"

"Not sure."

"Look, Kyle, I have a friend. It just so happens he's visiting right now. He's from New York. He's gay and works as a counselor at an AIDS center."

There was utter silence on the other end of the line.

"You mind if I give him your number?"

After about a year of silence, Kyle said, "Yeah, okay, Ms. Reif."

I couldn't make up for my lack of sensitivity, but at least I could put Kyle in touch with someone with resources, someone who could help him think things through, someone who could stop him from sliding into the darkness I heard in his voice.

When I gave my therapist friend Kyle's number, he explained that confidentiality would apply once he called. I was stunned to find out that when my friend went back to New York, Kyle went with him. It seemed an unlikely series of events—a star student, a therapist friend, a ticket to New York purchased by someone who cared.

Sometimes, success in the classroom is measured not by what you know about teaching but how you live your life. I always told the students that writing was thinking on paper. What I didn't tell them was how much I learned by reading their work.

When I turned my grades in that semester, there was an A in the empty square by Kyle's final grade. He was an accomplished writer. His lessons in life were irrefutable. Though my misgivings about that knock on my classroom door were real enough, I learned more about options that semester than I'd learned in my whole teaching life.

Orange Hair

By Cassandra W. Andre

With eyes half closed, Carl slumped over his desk, his head drooping over his crossed arms, while activity buzzed around him. His teacher told him to participate, he ignored her. She threatened to send him to the principal's office, he shrugged his shoulders. In a rural school of mostly Mexican migrant children, Carl stood out with his pale skin and thick hair so blonde it seemed almost white. Soft beige freckles ran wild over his arms but only tiptoed lightly across his small nose. Unlike the other children, he showed little interest in school activities, hid behind a sullen and uncooperative mask, and had few friends. He wasn't even eleven yet.

In the early 1970s I was living in a rural area of California at the northern tip of Monterey County and teaching at the local elementary school. The district brass had an idea that if our students participated in a "beautification program," their older siblings might be less likely to vandalize the school grounds. They asked me to oversee the program.

I planned several projects. My budget consisted of $50. With that I bought brushes, then spent the remainder on small cans of bright-colored paint of the type designed for sign painters.

Next I went to paint stores asking them to donate any of their cans of incorrectly mixed colors. Most stores were glad to unload their mistakes. We needed lots of paint so the kids could thoroughly cover the playground equipment, trash cans, and designs that we had planned for the asphalt. Small amounts of bright colors would then be used for highlights. The muddy mis-mixed colors made perfect backgrounds. Simple designs done in the bright colors contrasted perfectly.

A section cut out of the asphalt playground had a large, old, wooden boat partially sunken into the sand filling the play area. My next project consisted of painting the boat. The group of students for this class included Carl.

I passed the brushes and cans out, giving him a full quart of an ugly but distinctive orange paint. Displaying uncharacteristic enthusiasm, Carl asked to paint a specific section of the boat. No one else cared where they worked so I told him to go ahead and get started. While helping the rest of the students, I heard my name called. I turned. Carl stood shaking, almost in tears.

"Mrs. Andre," he sounded ready to panic. "I spilled my paint."

I told him not to worry but that he did need to wash the paint off himself. He didn't move. Tears began to run down his cheeks mingling with the paint.

"Carl, I am not angry or even upset with you. You just had an accident. We all have accidents. You must go wash off, though, because that paint sets up very quickly. So, please, go rinse the paint off."

A grin broke across what had been a sad, fearful face and he ran off.

The Carl who returned looked much like an Oompa Loompa, one of the orange-skinned creatures Willy Wonka had rescued from Loompaland and given a home at the Wonka chocolate factory. I realized his hair was as orange as his hands and arms, clothing and shoes. Previously, I hadn't noticed that he'd soaked himself so efficiently. I'd been too involved with the frightened child and assuring him he had nothing to fear. Wisely, all my students had been told to wear old clothes and shoes.

"Do you have any paint left?"

"Yes."

"Then finish painting."

Most importantly, his demeanor had changed, he seemed more self-assured. For the first time, I saw Carl smiling. The next day he greeted me as I arrived. Strutting, he proudly showed off his hair and talked about it remaining orange forever.

"Mrs. Andre! Mrs. Andre, I like my hair this color, don't you? I'm gonna keep it just like this forever. Yes, forever. Mrs. Andre, you like it, don't you?"

He also mentioned that he didn't get in trouble at home for spilling the paint. Until his orange hair grew out, he wore it like a badge of honor.

This change of behavior fascinated me so I asked other teachers and the principal about him. Gradually I gathered bits and pieces of information, and by combining these inquiries with casual conversations I had with the child, I discovered a history of abuse.

His parents didn't need a reason, but if he got in trouble at school that meant that he would suffer severely that evening. The round burn marks that I had noticed on his arms were from his dad punishing him with lit cigarettes. I also found out that the paint occurrence was the first time he had an accident that had not been first disciplined at school and then sadistically punished at home. He now knew that not all mistakes resulted in dire consequences.

That small incident made a huge difference in his behavior at school. He occasionally took chances, and as he gained confidence, he became bolder and more successful.

He told me, "Mrs. Andre, I like coming to school now. Learning is fun. I'm not dumb and stupid like everyone said."

For the rest of the time Carl attended that school, I made time to talk to him, hear about his achievements and talk of the pride I felt in knowing him. Of course, the abuse at home continued, even after the conversations I had with his parents telling them of his great improvement. This all happened before teachers were allowed to report abuse and have children protected. Still, I know that no matter what life challenges Carl has been given, he has the memory of a time when he knew he had value.

Unconditional value.

I was unable to follow Carl's progress. I do not know if he stayed in the area and attended local schools. My greatest concern was his home environment and whether he could withstand the abuse long enough to graduate. I never saw him again after he left the elementary school but, obviously, I've thought of him, and wished him well. He deserved a better life.

Because of changes in societal attitudes since I worked with Carl, teachers are not just encouraged, but required by law to report suspected abuse, and the state agencies who monitor such cases take child abuse in the home far more seriously than they did back then. Thank goodness, now there's something that can be done for the "next Carl" to come along.

Friends, Romans, Countrymen!

By Amy Shore

*F*riends, Romans, Country-
men! Lend me your ears!
I come to praise my freshmen!
Today was the day my fourteen-year-old students
donned togas and sandals in class and recited from memory
Shakespeare's famous "funeral speech" delivered by Marc
Antony to a very volatile crowd stunned by the death of
Julius Caesar. My freshmen had two weeks to memorize
Shakespeare's words; they have been reading and analyzing
the tragedy in class for the past few weeks. Today was their
day in the spotlight, and there was an electric current in the
air as they prepared for recitation.

I walked into my classroom when the bell rang and,
instead of seeing students talking in their seats, I saw boys
and girls outfitting themselves in the sheets they found in
their families' linen closets. Around their school uniforms

they wrapped and twisted white sheets, flowered sheets, striped sheets, and even a multicolored terry cloth towel. Curtain ties were draped across their waists and a few had laurel leaf crowns on top of their heads. Most wore sandals on their bare feet as discarded shoes and socks littered my classroom. One student even brought a bust of Caesar for inspiration!

Once they were fashioned like Romans, they nervously fidgeted in their seats and awaited their turn to recite Antony's funeral oration that had been memorized by their parents and generations before them and will be recited by generations to come. One by one each took his or her place in front of the classroom and recited the speech, at times stumbling over a phrase or a word that isn't part of our lingo anymore. Across each student's face fear flashed as his or her mind went blank and stage fright squeezed each heart for a moment or two. I gently prodded with three or four words, and then life returned to the student's eyes as he or she belted out the famous lines. When each uttered the last word, a sense of accomplishment was framed in a smile as the class applauded another performance! What a relief when it was over!

It's not easy getting up in front of one's peers when one is trying to survive the awkwardness of adolescence. It's really not easy standing before one's peers in a toga and sandals. Yet my students were brave and persevered! And they created a memory from high school that they will forever cherish. (And if they happen to forget, I took some pictures of them that will grace the pages of the yearbook!)

My students taught themselves something beyond what Shakespeare tries to convey in his play. They realized they could accomplish something they thought, originally, was impossible. ("You want us to memorize that whole page?!" they cried when I first assigned the project.) Words foreign to them spilled from their lips, and an energy and power lifted their souls. They discovered that they could actually memorize a big chunk of writing. They could stand before their peers and survive! They could do it. Heck, they could do anything!

And they triumphed! And for forty-five minutes today, Shakespeare, from Heaven, was smiling, too!

Write What You Know

By Michael Bracken

The first time that I taught a continuing education course, I didn't know what to expect. I was an inexperienced young adult in my twenties, had sold a few short stories, and thought I knew everything about writing fiction and getting published. I presumed everyone who enrolled in my class would desire publication just as much as I did.

They didn't.

That first evening, I faced about a dozen students—many of them women of my mother's and grandmother's generations—who had enrolled for a variety of reasons, from "always liked writing" to "needed a reason to get out of the house and this looked like fun."

I had intended to teach my students how to prepare and submit manuscripts to editors, but none of the students were ready for publication. Instead, we discussed the elements of a good story—setting, plot, dialog, characterization, and story arc. Each week the students brought their half-realized or stillborn manuscripts to class and we discussed their work. We read about Wild West gunfights, scary things in the basement, epic space battles, and Marge's stories about an abused woman.

In her mid-thirties, Marge was attractive even though she wore her makeup a little thick and her ill-fitting clothes appeared to come from a thrift store. She always sat in the back of the classroom, in the desk closest to the exit. She rarely spoke and she never made eye contact, even when I spoke directly to her. About halfway through the semester, we started moving the desks into a circle to facilitate discussion, and Marge still managed to distance herself from the rest of the class.

Character motivation became important to the students. Why did aging Sheriff Cartwright agree to a gunfight at high noon? Why was seven-year-old Billy afraid of the strange sounds coming from the basement? Why did Commander Armstrong battle the six-tentacled Venusians to save the three-eyed Martians? And why didn't Marge's unnamed protagonist leave her abusive husband?

I challenged the class to reexamine their stories. "It isn't enough that your characters do things," I explained. "It's also important for the readers to understand why they do the things they do. What's their motivation?"

As the semester wore on, we learned that the sheriff was battling certain death from a wasting disease and had chosen suicide by gunfight rather than a slow death in bed; that Billy's stepfather had convinced him the rattle of the coal-fired furnace was the sound of monsters that lived in the basement; and that a three-eyed Martian had once saved Commander Armstrong's sister from "a fate worse than death."

We never learned why Marge's unnamed protagonist suffered her husband's abuse without leaving him. Each week Marge brought a new manuscript to share, and each week the story was the same. Marge changed the setting—sometimes events took place in the kitchen and other times in the bedroom—and she changed the particular method of abuse from a slap in the face to a punch in the gut, but her stories always ended the same: her unnamed protagonist crying alone after her drunken husband passed out.

I grew frustrated with Marge. Because there are no grades, what students gain from a continuing education course is proportionate to the amount of effort they expend, and all of the students except Marge improved as the weeks passed. Although they were still a long way from publication, the students had grasped the elements of a good story and had begun to incorporate setting, plot, dialog, and characterization into their work. They had even begun to grasp that a story arc required a beginning, a middle, and an end, with characters that changed from the time the story began to the time the story ended. Not Marge. She continued to write the same incomplete story she'd been writing at the beginning of the semester.

I was still young enough to believe I knew everything, so I caught Marge in the hallway after the last class of the semester and made one last attempt to drive home some of the key points her classmates had grasped.

"You can't write the same thing over and over," I told her. "Your characters must change. Your protagonist—the woman with no name that you keep writing about—has to do *something* to change her life. If she doesn't change, there's no story. If you want to be a writer, you must master the story arc—beginning, middle, and end. You must give your characters valid motivation for their actions, and they must change during the course of the story."

She flinched once during my tirade, when I used my hands to draw a story arc in the air, and even then I didn't see anything beyond my own narrow view of the world.

My first continuing education teaching experience ended that day in February 1985, but I taught the same course each following semester through spring 1988. My approach to the material changed to accommodate each new group of students, but it was my life outside the classroom that changed the most.

During the next few years I discovered how little I actually understood about the world around me. Because so much of my knowledge came from stories where problems were always resolved by the last page, I struggled with the harsh realities of marriage, parenthood, and full-time employment. I learned that reality didn't have a plot and that lessons we learned were hard won and often ambiguous, not handed to us like the neat little morals at the end of Aesop's Fables.

Years later, long after I had forgotten about the students in my first continuing education class, I ran into Marge at a grocery store. She'd lost weight, wore clothes that actually fit her figure, and whatever makeup she wore was understated.

"I left him," she said.

"Left who?"

"My husband. You were right."

"About what?" I asked. Then I remembered her story and I began to put the pieces together. I understood what I couldn't understand then: Marge had been writing about herself, and she couldn't write the ending to her story because she didn't know how it ended. Neither did I until that chance meeting in the grocery store.

"After your class, I finally had the courage to stand up for myself," Marge explained. She had her own apartment, a job, and was attending college part-time.

I had incorrectly believed everyone enrolled in my continuing education classes desired publication, but Marge's reasons for writing had nothing to do with writing at all. She'd been writing to be heard. She'd been writing for her life.

And she'd finally written the ending she deserved.

Seeing Through Tom

By Joyce Grant-Smith

I took my teaching training as an early elementary educator. Surprisingly, a few years later my convoluted career path led me into a middle school, teaching grade six. Instead of zipping zippers, wiping noses, and dealing with the management of other body fluids, I was coping with emerging hormones. It was different, but I found that kids were kids, and big or small, they all needed kindness and guidance, and I enjoyed them all.

My second year at the middle school, the principal found out that my university background was in English. He was desperate to find a grade eight English teacher. He asked me if I would give it a try.

Grade eight is the black hole of education. Students are in that twilight zone between the enthusiastic elementary school years and the earnest senior high years. Hormones have taken over their thought processes so their attention spans are approximately that of two-year-olds. Their attitudes are remarkably similar to those of two-year-olds as well, but while the Terrible Twos say, "No!" the grade eights say, "So?" It takes a very special person to cope with grade eight students, and I wasn't at all sure I was such a person.

The principal's need for an English teacher outweighed my misgivings, and so in September, I faced two grade eight classes each day. The classes were large, with over thirty students enrolled in each. The desks were jammed in my room; the students were packed in like sardines. Forget trying to keep the "bad actors" separated. I'd need an octagonal shaped classroom to have a corner for each character. Lanky adolescent legs hung out in the aisles. The situation looked pretty bleak.

I bravely read up on best practices for middle school English classroom management. I experimented with methods and motivational ideas. I survived from day to day.

Once I started to get to know my students, things began to improve. They soon learned that I wasn't a teacher who would put up with much foolishness. But they also learned that I had a sympathetic ear and I was quick to give hugs if that was what they wanted.

I had one student who had recently moved into the area. He was proving to be a bit of a challenge. I'll call him Tom. He sat up front, near the door, with his long legs sprawled out toward me. He was a handsome young man, but his face was usually twisted into a mocking sneer.

Around the school Tom was getting the reputation of being a "smart-ass." His eyes challenged the teacher to just try to make him work. He often had a glib comment during the teachers' lectures, and he rarely did his homework.

I thought I saw something behind Tom's tough-guy routine. Self-doubt, perhaps. Or fear. Or the desire to fit in somehow, even if it was in a negative way.

I started to push Tom a little in class. I'd ask him questions about what we'd been reading. I'd make him think. I gave him detentions if he didn't get his writing assignments passed in to me.

At first, there was resistance, of course, and a little hostility. But I started getting some work out of Tom.

His writing surprised me. Granted, he couldn't spell to save his life. And grammar and punctuation were not his strong suits. But could that boy tell a story! His plots were carefully woven, and his climaxes masterful.

"I love this ending," I wrote on one story. "It was a complete surprise! And it tied everything together beautifully. Please watch spelling, though."

He sidled up to me after class, the story in his hand. "You really liked this?" he asked.

"Oh, yes," I enthused. "It was great. That twist in the plot where the bell tolled was well done."

He kind of shook his head. "But the spelling . . . "

I smiled. "We do have to work on that," I said. "But spelling is just a small part of writing. Your ideas are very good. You just need to polish the finished product a bit more."

He walked out of the classroom with a lopsided grin, his story carefully tucked into his binder.

The grade eights were expected to pass in a piece of creative writing every two weeks, and from then on, Tom always had something for me. He started to write for the love of writing.

About this time, the school had parent-teacher interviews. Tom's folks came in.

It turned out that Tom lived with his grandparents. They did not tell me what had happened to Tom's parents, whether they were dead or they had run out on him, and I didn't ask. But knowing Tom had lost them, one way or another, gave me some insight as to why he put on the tough-guy mask when he arrived at our school.

"We're pleased with Tommy's English mark," the grandmother said to me.

Tom, sitting next to her, winced at being called "Tommy."

"He seems to be doing quite well in your class," the grandfather agreed.

We discussed Tom's progress, having a nice chat. All at once, Tom blurted sarcastically, "Maybe you'd like to come to our house for tea some afternoon, Mrs. GS, since you and my folks get along so well." He'd heard about all the positive things that he could stand about himself for a while, I guess.

My response was, "Tea would be lovely."

He had to laugh.

In my class, his glib comments changed into dry witticisms that I really enjoyed. We shared many jokes that went over the heads of several of his classmates.

Tom's interest in English started to spill over into his other subjects. The math teacher mentioned to me that Tom was actually starting to do his homework. His science teacher noted that he must have studied for his last test, because he pulled off a decent mark. He would never be a scholar, but he began to get passing grades in his courses. By the time June rolled around, Tom had gained a passing grade in all his courses and was on his way to high school.

Tom came to see me the last day of classes. He found me during a rare quiet moment, when I wasn't busy with other students.

"I just wanted to come and say thanks," he said. "I don't think I would have gotten through this year without you."

"Oh, Tom, it's been wonderful teaching you," I replied.

"You know, I was a new kid here and everything. I didn't know how I was going to cope. I figured I'd get creamed. But maybe if I was dumb and the class clown, I would fit in." He looked at me in the eye. "But you saw through me.

You pushed me to work hard. You're a good teacher. I think you're a good friend, too."

Those are words a teacher lives for. They filled my heart.

That wasn't the end of my relationship with Tom, though.

Tom took a part-time job at the grocery store where I shopped and he made it a point of being my carry-out guy so we could chat on the way out to my car.

One day he was worried about a science project that he had to complete. He had no idea how to get started on it. I invited him to stop by my classroom the next day and I'd help him with it.

"You mean it?" he asked.

"Sure. I'd be happy to give you a hand."

He did drop by and we worked out his rough draft together.

Another time, he was really excited. "I won my division at the provincial wrestling championships on the weekend, Mrs. GS!" he crowed.

"That's super!" I congratulated him.

"The guy from Halifax was really tough. He had some bad holds. But I pinned him in the end."

One summer day as I was shopping, I heard Tom in the next aisle. He was hiccuping. Not cute little polite hiccups, but nasty jarring ones.

"Hey, Mrs. (hic!) GS!" he greeted me. "Know how (hic!) to get rid of (hic!) hiccups? I've (hic!) had them all (hic!) afternoon."

"Yes, I do," I said. "Do you trust me?"

He nodded, but gave me a look that said, "Now what are you up to?"

"You're a wrestler, so you know how to ground your feet, right?" I asked.

He hiccuped and nodded.

"Okay, ground your feet, take a couple of deep breaths, and pass your hand in front of your chest as if you were brushing the hiccups away."

I could tell Tom thought I'd really lost it this time, but he did as I instructed. And the hiccups stopped. The look that came over his face was priceless. If I'd waved a magic wand and said, "Begone hiccups!" I don't think he'd have been more in awe.

Tom often bounced ideas off me, or just talked out problems he was having.

He didn't always make good decisions (what teenager does?) but he had a pretty good head on his shoulders and he kept his sense of humor. I liked watching him grow up into a young man.

Finally, when he completed the requirements for high school, he came to see me. I was sitting at my classroom desk at the end of a long June day, marking papers. I smiled and greeted him as he stepped through the door.

"Hey, Tom, how are things?"

"Good. I came to bring you this." He passed me a ticket for the grade twelve graduation ceremony. Graduates were given four tickets for reserved seats for graduation night. Usually these went to parents and grandparents.

I looked up into his earnest face. "Are you sure, Tom? You don't have someone else you want to give this to?"

He shook his head and gave me that lopsided grin of his. "I don't think I'd have made it this far without you, Mrs. GS. You got me started on the right foot back in grade eight, and you've been there for me lots of times since then. I'm always coming to you for advice. So, I really want you to be there when I graduate."

With tears in my eyes, I said, "Tom, I wouldn't miss it for anything. Thank you."

I watched proudly as Tom walked across the stage to receive his diploma that June night. At the reception following the ceremony, I searched him out. I didn't want to take time away from his family and friends, but I had a little gift for him. A journal, so he would keep on writing.

"I'm proud of you," I said. I hugged him and left him to his celebrations.

Tom moved away to another province. He did come to see me once more after that. It was a couple of years ago. I was at school, sitting at my desk, when he walked in. He looked kind of worn.

He sat down and told me that his grandfather had passed away. He had come home for the funeral. We talked for a long while, about his grandfather, his job working in a supermarket, and the woman he was in love with. Then he left.

I don't know if Tom still writes. Part of me hopes that he puts pen to paper, and feels that author's thrill of a well-turned phrase.

There are times when I wonder why I still teach, why I work with adolescents day in and day out. And then, I think about Tom and how I really did make a difference in that young lad's life.

And I know exactly why I still teach.

Goodwill Cranes

By Dianna Graveman

*R*egardless of their political beliefs, it is probably safe to say most people wish for world peace. One of the nice things about teaching elementary school is that little children not only wish for peace, they are still young enough to believe it can be achieved.

In February 2003, my fourth-grade students read *Sadako and the Thousand Paper Cranes*, by Elizabeth Coerr. Sadako Sasaki was born in Japan in 1943, just two years before the atom bomb was dropped on Hiroshima on August 6, 1945. When she was eleven years old, she became dizzy and fainted while running a race. Like many other Japanese people exposed to radiation from the bomb, she was diagnosed with leukemia.

There is a Japanese legend which says that anyone who folds a thousand paper cranes will get one wish. Sadako began folding the paper cranes, but she became seriously ill before completing a thousand. Her friends and classmates finished folding the cranes for her.

A monument to Sadako and all of the people who died from the atomic bomb blast was erected in 1958 in Hiroshima Peace Park. At the top of the monument is a likeness of Sadako holding a paper crane, and an inscription at the bottom reads:

This is our cry,
This is our prayer
Peace in the world

After reading the book in the late winter of 2003, my students and I found information on the Internet about a school project that has grown internationally over the last several years. Classes from all over the world read Sadako's story and fold a thousand paper cranes, string them together, and mail them to Japan as a symbol of peace and an offering of goodwill between the children and their nations. Thousands of brightly colored cranes from around the globe are then placed at the foot of Sadako's monument for the celebration of Peace Day on August 6th each year.

My class decided to participate in the worldwide project, and we soon undertook the daunting task of constructing one thousand origami cranes to send to Japan. At first, the children were enthusiastic, and little fingers flew through the making of many paper cranes. Every spare minute was devoted to making more cranes and stringing them together so they could be rolled up and boxed. Within a month's time, the students had made and strung over seven hundred cranes. But in the cool, cloudy days of late February and early March, some of the enthusiasm began to wane. We had moved on to other projects. Spring was coming, and the children's minds were on fresh air, sunshine, and playing outdoors.

On March 20th, the day the *St. Louis Post Dispatch's* front page headline read, "Strategic Strikes Open War on Iraq," most children came to school with questions and concerns. Some were worried about family members or friends who were in the military. A few of them were concerned for the children of Iraq. After our morning discussion, the class decided they really wanted to finish those cranes that very day. For forty minutes, there was very little noise in the classroom except for the sound of crisp paper squares being shaped into perfect little birds.

Soon our box was overflowing with cranes, and we stopped to count. When it appeared that we had almost reached our goal of one thousand, the stringing of the cranes began in earnest. "Eight hundred!" a boy's voice rang out as he finished his string of one hundred cranes.

"This string is done!" called another voice a few minutes later.

As the final one hundred cranes were slipped one by one on to the last string, the children began to count in unison: "Nine hundred eighty-nine! Nine hundred ninety!"

A calm stillness enveloped the classroom when the one thousandth crane was placed on the string. "We need to make a wish," someone whispered.

I watched as several sets of ten-year-old eyes closed, brows furrowed in concentration, while the children made their wishes. A few of the children clasped their hands, as if in prayer. I knew in my heart that many of us were wishing for the same thing: Peace among children, among people, among nations. Peace in our world.

When the wishes were made and the eyes were open, I announced, "Now you can cheer!" I opened my classroom door so that the whole school could hear the roar of exultation rise up from Room 26. There were pats on the back and high fives all around. Two little girls hugged. A teacher passing by our classroom stopped to applaud.

The dismissal bell rang, and the jubilant children tumbled out of school into the sunshine. Once more, my classroom was silent. I placed our last rolled-up string of cranes in the box and closed the lid, preparing the package for its trip to Japan. But I wasn't done. This box needed something else. What? I clutched a thick marker, poised over the box's lid, thinking.

Turning suddenly, I noticed two fourth-grade faces peering at me from the doorway. "What else?" I asked. "What should we say?"

"How about that thing from the statue?" said one. "You know, about peace."

Perfect. Across the top of the box, in large letters, I printed:

This is our cry
This is our prayer
Peace in the world

The pair nodded solemnly and slipped from view. Then in the stillness of the school room, with splashes of late afternoon sun brightening the shadows and lifting my heart, I bowed my head.

Wake-Up Call

By Melissa S. Bennett

stood in front of the crowded classroom feeling overwhelmed. This was my first teaching job out of college and if I had to describe myself in one word it would be *naive*. They stared at me and I stared at them, wondering how I was going to reach out to them. How would I make them love and appreciate art the way that I did? However, teaching these kids art appreciation was not my ultimate goal in being a teacher. I wanted to reach out to my students and make a difference in their lives in some way.

Before I knew it, the days had passed quickly and I found myself finishing off the first marking period. Soon I would receive all new students for another nine weeks. Although the weeks had flown by, I did not really feel as successful as I had hoped I would be.

I had thought teaching would be so easy. The kids would be so excited to do art. After all, I had been that way as a student. I quickly realized this was not the case. Classroom management was going to be the area that I would have the biggest difficulty with. I felt that lesson plans and keeping control were taking up all of my time. I was not connecting with my students the way I had always imagined I would.

As the second marking period rolled around I had a blank spot in my schedule for the rest of the year. When I approached the principal about it, he explained I would hold an advanced art class for the most artistically gifted eighth graders to prepare them for their high school art classes.

"Pick between ten and fifteen of the top eighth graders," he explained to me.

"But, I only had one eighth-grade class so far," I protested. "The rest were seventh. I don't know enough of the eighth graders to be able to do that."

"What do you have this marking period?"

"All eighth grade."

"Good," he said. "Wait a couple weeks then pick from them."

That sounded reasonable, so I agreed.

I soon realized this was going to be more of a challenge than I had anticipated. A couple of the students were obvious choices for the advanced class. Their talent amazed me. But the rest were tricky. How do you pick out of 250 students? Especially when I was just starting to learn their names. I studied all of their projects looking for skill and creativity. After a couple weeks, I completed a list of thirteen students that I thought would benefit from this program. One boy named Andy made me hesitate. He was definitely lacking some of the skill and knowledge of art principles that the other students possessed. I eventually put in his name because he really seemed to have the interest and the creativity.

I soon realized that I really looked forward to this period each day. The students involved were thrilled to be there. In fact, I had other students begging to be let in (although I think that was mostly to get out of one of their other classes). Andy was particularly enthusiastic about being part of this special class. He tried very hard and often told me how happy he was to be in it. I would smile and nod at him, but not really take it all in.

One day, though, Andy's comment bothered me a bit. It was near the end of the year and as a last project, the students were designing T-shirts. My students were spread throughout the room finishing various projects. Andy was with me in the back of the room. He was helping me get the shirts ready by putting cardboard in between the front and back so the design would not transfer through.

"Art is the only thing I am good at," the tall, black-clad fourteen-year-old told me.

I tried to reassure him, "Oh, I'm sure that is not true." I said this absently, because I was actually concentrating more on what I was doing at the time. I was in the middle of ironing designs onto T-shirts. I had a pile of them to get done that period, but I also wanted to get them done right.

"No, it really is," he said. "Art is the only thing I feel like I can do. I hope I can do it as a career someday."

"I'm sure you will," I told him as I began another shirt.

"Do you mind if I go to the bathroom and put on my shirt?" Andy asked as I handed him his.

I smiled at him. "No, not at all."

Andy loved to design cartoon characters. He had worked hard on this particular one. I was happy he was pleased with it. When he came back in to display his shirt, I complimented him on what a good job he had done with the design. Then I noticed some marking around his neck. I had seen him often wear choker-style necklaces, so my first thought was that he'd had an allergic reaction to one. I went back to my ironing. Andy continued to talk to me.

"The only problem with this shirt is that everyone can see my neck," he murmured.

Not really thinking much of it (being as naive as I was), I asked, "Oh, what happened?"

"I tried to hang myself last night," he told me nonchalantly. "But my mom caught me. She made me go to the hospital and back to the therapist."

I felt as thought the school was about to crash down on me. I managed to lift the iron and set it aside so I wouldn't burn the shirt.

"Oh, Andy," was about all I got out, when the bell rang.

"See you tomorrow!" He waved and was out the door before I could say a word.

I went to the principal and told him the situation. Andy was already receiving help, but deep down I felt like I had let Andy down. I was in shock. I had spent almost my entire first year as a teacher preparing lessons intended to impress coworkers and worrying about the students throwing colored pencils that I had almost forgotten that these kids were people. I had lost sight of my goal to reach out to them.

Andy made me realize that the most important thing about being a teacher was the students. Over the next few years I learned that sometimes the best classroom management plan you can have is to get the respect of the students around you. They will respond far better to you giving them a little bit of your time than they ever will to you posting a ton of rules and constantly assigning them detention.

I received a letter from Andy the following year thanking me for putting him in that special class. But I felt that I should have been the one who was thanking him.

Enrichment

By Jo E. Gray

Charles stood in the doorway, not quite sure he wanted to take part in the elective program known by the junior high students as "Reading Enrichment."

I knew it as remedial reading and this was the first week program.

The students qualifying for the program were given the option of coming to the class or staying in study hall.

"Please come in and have a seat," I encouraged Charles.

With a slow, labored walk, the tall, blond eighth grader took a seat in the back of the classroom and fixed his stare on me.

I began the class by asking each student to write his or her name at the top of a blank sheet of paper, followed by a brief history of a problem with which he or she required help. I should have made the assignment clearer. I should have mentioned the problem must be an academic one.

Following his name, Charles had written one word—"Dad."

The next morning I arrived at school early so I could talk to Charles's school counselor. I needed to know more about this sad student. Why did he never smile? Why did he stay to himself?

From a broken home, Charles was an only child who had been more or less left to his own devices. His school records indicated he was smart enough yet he had repeated an earlier grade.

The counselor told me Charles had more problems than a broken home. His older sister had died in an automobile accident and his father had turned to alcohol.

When Charles showed up for class that day he was less timid and more curious. He showed interest in the new head phones and various audio equipment. This reading class was different. There was none of the then-typical approach to reading classes: sitting in a circle with each student taking his turn at oral reading.

He found an empty desk nearer mine. Still, he watched me with a look of mistrust and didn't take part in group activities.

By the end of the first month, Charles, like others, had shown no progress in oral or silent reading. Hoping to inspire some of the students to read more, I announced a project open only to them.

"We are going to put on a three-act play," I announced with all the enthusiasm I could gather. "And, if we do it well enough, the entire school will be invited to see our performance on stage."

I distributed a version of *The Honeymooners*, a popular television series of the 1950s and '60s, geared for students of this age, and asked each child to read it and decide the part he or she wanted. Auditions were to be the following Monday.

I noticed Charles did not take a copy of the play. I asked that he remain after class so we could talk about his decision. I had already made up my mind about his participation and the part he would have. I wanted him to take the role of Ralph Kramden, the role played by Jackie Gleason in the original TV series.

When I asked him why he didn't want to try out he replied, "It's dumb."

"You won't know it's dumb if you don't read it," I told him. "And, I was hoping you would want the lead part. You would be great."

Seeing I had his interest I tried again. "Why won't you at least take it home and read it with your dad?"

Charles shifted his weight from one foot to the other as he stood looking at the floor.

"My dad doesn't want me having homework. He thinks school is stupid."

"So, that's it," I told myself.

I convinced Charles to read the play.

The following Monday, auditions were held. The students were excited. There were only a few who hadn't chosen to participate on stage. They worked hard first learning to read their roles and then memorizing them. Those who didn't want to be on stage were assigned roles as stagehands, scenery designers, etc.

Charles not only learned his role, he volunteered to go first. Once he had captured the spirit of Ralph Kramden, the overbearing bus driver, the other students agreed he should have the part. Charles took on a new personality as he helped others learn their parts. As he gained confidence, he became a willing participant in all class projects.

The play was a huge success. The principal decided there should be an evening performance to which parents would be invited. As a class project, students designed and wrote invitations to parents. While his father didn't attend the performance, Charles was excited to see his grandmother in the audience.

The test scores at the end of the year revealed Charles had progressed beyond grade level in reading comprehension. But, as his teacher, I found the most rewarding part of having Charles in the class was the growth he had made toward accepting himself. He had achieved the recognition of his peers as well as that of at least one family member.

He accepted his eighth-grade diploma with confidence. I think I noticed a smile as he turned toward the audience.

His dad was in the second row.

Ten-Minute Tommy and the Seven-Minute Mile

By Joel Thomas Hoffschneider

A murmur of doubt rippled through the crowd assembled along the dried grass perimeter of the track. Could it be done? Tommy had started to struggle. His breathing came harder, his strides shorter. Still, he didn't stop. He pushed forward with the same determination that had gotten him through the difficult divorce of his parents, and the years of abuse from children who didn't understand him and therefore feared him. Given that Tommy suffered from autism, a glandular disorder that pushed his weight well over 250 pounds, and Fibrous Dysplasia (a skeletal disorder that causes expansion and abnormal development of the fibrous, or connective, tissue within the bone), it was amazing he could even walk.

A perfectionist with a genius IQ, twelve-year-old Tommy was nothing if not determined. Every day he would join the other sixth-grade boys at lunchtime who worked on their mile time. As each young man achieved the goal of 7:32, the group of twelve became nine, then seven, then four. Finally, Tommy was the only one left. It was the last chance that he would have before year's end. For two months, he had been fixated on one number: 7:32. Seven minutes, thirty-two seconds. The magical time that would earn him the President's Physical Fitness award.

Quite a big deal if you're the only boy in the sixth grade of St. Mathew's Middle School who has *not* gotten the patch. For Tommy, it was three and a half laps in 7:32 to the top of "Fitness Award Mountain."

As his sixth-grade teacher, I'd been observing Tommy for some six months now. I sensed that something was different today. Maybe it was because Tommy had actually stretched before the event, something he had flatly refused to do in the past. Most of his classmates had remained indifferent during the first lap. It was well known that Tommy's best was around 9 minutes. As I watched him, a chill ran up my spine. Whatever it was, the fact that he hadn't stopped at the second turn, or the third turn, had gotten my attention. When he crossed the line of lap one, I glanced at the amazing time on my watch: 1:56. Looks of mild interest traveled from student to student. As lap two came and went, the stir became a wave, a rising blur of voices with one common thought: Tommy had a chance.

The twenty-three kids of his class had gathered at the far turn. The chant slowly grew to one intense, rhythmic voice: "Tommy! Tommy!" Just a few minutes before, he had been nothing except the heavy, temperamental boy that people avoided. Now, with all the odds stacked against him, pushing himself further than he ever had before, he had even drawn the attention of parents crossing the parking lot and faculty returning from lunch.

Lap three: 6:50. As I watched his knees buckling with every stride, I knew that the end was near. At half a lap, his breathing had become tight and labored. His face was crimson with effort. A pang of dread twisted my stomach. I jogged alongside him for a second or two. He vigorously waved me off. It was clear that he wanted no help.

The numbers on the stopwatch kept whisking by beneath the circling hand. As he rounded the final turn, seven minutes came and went. Then it happened, the sight of the gathered students at the finish line, not shouting at him but for him, unleashed within him the heart of a champion. A heart that had been locked down by years of self-doubt and fear now beat a strong tattoo. He was their hero. If they thought that he could do it, then he would not disappoint them. Tommy didn't just keep going . . . he started sprinting! The clock whirred, the class roared; Tommy puffed across the finish line in 7:28. He had made it!

Teacher Miracles

With all of the burdens that had been heaped on his young body, he might as well have been Roger Bannister breaking the four-minute mile. Beyond the celebration that followed his triumphant run, something much more important had occurred than just the earning of a patch that would soon be forgotten in some drawer somewhere: Tommy's view of himself changed forever.

Every teacher who straps on a slide rule and their trusty "six shooter" color-marking pen lives for moments like these. We get up every day, eager to see our students achieve, to watch them conquer impossible odds and in the end, find their true selves. Tommy hadn't only inspired an entire class of students to push themselves further, harder, and faster. He had reminded them all that within *every* young person we meet is the potential for greatness. As a teacher, it's been my privilege to help my students create ways they can sprint past their challenges and triumph over their handicaps.

On this day, "Too-Slow" Tommy became "Triumphant" Tommy. Six years later, "Class President" Tommy graduated from high school the same way he had finished that race, at the top of his class.

Life in Twenty-Five Easy Lessons

By Carol Kilgore

From the moment we pop from Mom's belly until the day we join The Big Guy in the Sky, we learn. We receive formal instruction from teachers from pre-K through Ph.D., but this formal instruction is only a small fraction of all the things we learn.

Consider:

Lesson One. On the day we're born, we learn that if someone smacks us, it's going to hurt.

Lesson Two. On this same day, we learn that if someone holds us, the hurt goes away.

Lesson Three. No matter how bad a face we make or how many times we spit it out, we still have to eat our spinach.

Lesson Four. Haircuts don't hurt.

Fast forward ten years. It's cool to be a kid—except for homework.

Lesson Five. We can't tell the teacher, "The dog ate my homework." Even if the other kids do laugh.

Lesson Six. The dog still loves us if we blame him for something he didn't do. Our best friend doesn't.

Lesson Seven. Some people do things better than we do, even when we give it our all. And sometimes we're the best.

Lesson Eight. It's fun to eat hot dogs in the rain.

Fast forward another ten years. I'm an adult. I can do what I want, when I want.

Lesson Nine. The world doesn't revolve around us.

Lesson Ten. We should have paid more attention in class.

Lesson Eleven. There's no spring break. Even worse, there's no summer-long vacation.

Lesson Twelve. Paychecks are nice.

Ten more years. Did you see her at the reunion?

Lesson Thirteen. Babies smell either really good . . . or really bad.

Lesson Fourteen. Toddlers are fast.

Lesson Fifteen. Sometimes it's necessary to step back and let children learn by doing.

Lesson Sixteen. Road trips build character.

Ten more. Where did that gray hair spring from?

Lesson Seventeen. Our teachers were never this young.

Lesson Eighteen. Homework never changes.

Lesson Nineteen. Children always find a way to surprise us.

Lesson Twenty. Adult vacations are wonderful.

OH MY GOD! I can't be fifty . . . and counting.

Lesson Twenty-One. Self-improvement classes are good things.

Lesson Twenty-Two. We are the person we see in the mirror—despite the yoga classes.

Lesson Twenty-Three. No matter how much we saved or how well we invested, retirement is expensive.

Lesson Twenty-Four. Weeds become wildflowers if we let them grow long enough.

And the most important lesson of all, the one we learn and relearn throughout life:

Lesson Twenty-Five. Whether we're five or fifty—younger or older—we're all teachers and we're all students at one time or another. Every day brings a chance to learn something new.

Learning to Read as a Late Bloomer in Oregon

By Dona J. Kirby

A few years ago, I moved to a small town in Oregon. While I was there, the local Home Health Care Coordinator asked me to serve as a substitute teacher. To say that I was startled would be putting it mildly. I had just spent the last fifteen years of my career in a private residential setting for severely/profoundly mentally and physically handicapped individuals.

That position involved education interspersed with detailed and arduous medical treatments for persons challenged because of birth trauma, accidents, genetic complications, and sometimes just bad luck. Every day I struggled to teach, right in the middle of recurring health crises that frequently rendered moot any advances my students made. I was looking forward to "regular" education or at least "regular" special ed, whatever that meant. Meanwhile, I was taking what I considered a well-deserved break in order to prepare myself for a new job teaching in either an elementary or middle school.

However, we had been living in our new home for nine months, my son was established in middle school, my husband was well acquainted with his new job, and my "taking time off for me" sojourn was getting tiresome. The Home Health Coordinator informed me that although services were typically provided in the home in this school district, I should consider a regular meeting at the local library since the family's involvement was complicated. When I asked her what I would be doing, she told me that I would be helping a young fourth-grade girl "catch up" with her reading after being ill. Naively enough, I thought this sounded like a simple task and agreed to help Lauren.

Prior to meeting Lauren I visited her elementary school, where her classroom teacher gave me vague directions and me told to "just see where she is and encourage her to do her best." She followed up this gem by favoring me with a fourth-grade textbook and a wan smile.

I showed up early to the local library at the appointed time and waited. Before long a very loud, large, unkempt—and as it turned out, opinionated—woman arrived with a young girl in tow. Sylvia, the mother, had arrived to "show" me what Lauren needed and was less than happy when I requested that she allow me time alone with her daughter.

I suggested we meet and discuss my plan the next day. After she "huffed" away, I was able to turn my attention to my new student. Lauren was small for her age with the brightest red hair and the largest freckles I had ever seen. "Hi," she said, "I'm Lauren. I just got over having leukemia and I don't know how to read. Mom told me you would teach me now."

Well, Lauren had not exaggerated; she could indeed not read, at all! Falsely, she had been told that once she was "done with leukemia" a teacher would teach her to read and she would be okay. No cautions were given that it would take time, it would be complicated by residual effects of chemotherapy, etc. So Lauren was ready to learn to read. Needless to say, my fourth-grade text was going to be of little use. Lauren and I headed for the library stacks to find our first textbook, a pre-primer book labeling household items.

The routine of the days that followed became predictable. Mom always arrived sure that today would be the day that she could stay and help. Each day she left resigned to the fact that Lauren and I were just as determined to do it on our own. We began our sessions with some writing and fine motor activities; reading was not the only thing that her leukemia had affected. Then we read. We took books that the library had two copies of so that we could read together. Lauren would read one page and I would read the next.

Something about the determination in that little girl was truly miraculous. We followed no research-based curriculum, we didn't scaffold our learning to build on previous lessons, and we didn't develop phonics or sight-word skills. The best I can define it is—and I know this is not educationally sound—we read. We read everything in sight, from Dr. Seuss to Beverly Cleary. She took books home and returned them two days later hungry for more.

Our first day together was in January of Lauren's fourth-grade year. By May she was reading and comprehending as a third grade, seventh month student (as measured by her first standardized test). I knew that I had done little more than provide the support and encouragement to do what she had announced to me that first day. Lauren was determined to read and to catch up. Leukemia had stolen two long, hard years from her life and she was done being left behind.

The year following found me teaching full time at the elementary school that Lauren attended as a fifth grader. The last day of school was bittersweet for me as it marked the end of a short, wonderful teaching experience in Oregon and my family was preparing to move to Washington.

At the end of that last day, Lauren ran up to me on the playground soaking wet from a water balloon fight and with freckles shining in the sunlight. "Don't be sad, Mrs. Kirby," she said. "You and I learned how to read together. You'll be fine when you go to your new school."

Staying Gold

By Kevin Klein

*A*s the principal stands up to start the ceremony, I glance around the small chapel. Almost all the chairs are taken, most of them by staff like me, some by people with VISITOR stickers on their shirts, and the rest by several of the students them-selves—or "clients," as we call them. Vanessa sits next to the podium in a cap and robe. We're all here to watch her graduate from high school.

Not very many kids get their own private graduation. What makes this ceremony even more special, though, is the work Vanessa has done for it. The high school program here is part of a residential treatment center for adolescents learning to deal with the most traumatic and unrelenting problems that people can face: abandonment, abuse, and addiction; anxiety, depression, and personality disorders.

For Vanessa, the domestic abuse she suffered as a young girl was compounded by the onset of bipolar disorder, and life became a struggle that she couldn't handle on her own. She describes that emotional crisis in this poem:

"How It Started"
Used to be the perfect daughter
Who filled every room with laughter
At thirteen she became lost
Wanted to fit in at whatever cost
Sick of always being good
Never in a bad mood
One day she lost it all
Her friends started not to call
All alone and by herself
She tried to become someone else
She tried to take her own life
But scared of that decision's price
Struggled to get through each day
And every night she would pray
What did I do that would make
My life become so hard to fake
Had to get in really deep
All of my past started to creep
But I realized it wasn't me
Not my fault, everyone could see
What I tried to secretly keep

Hate the hand I was dealt
You will never know how it felt
All my emotions were all bottled
And finally my personal hell exploded.

Vanessa's first dark days started almost four years ago. Her challenges grew from bad to worse until she made it to this treatment center two and a half years later. Many kids have a difficult entry into the center, but Vanessa's began before she actually arrived. When the school's pair of escorts went to pick her up from the hospital where she was staying she was upset, as most kids are, and wanted to run away from them, as many kids do. One escort restrained her from behind in a modified bear hug called the basket, and Vanessa pushed back against him with such force that the escort's backside put a crack in the Sheetrock wall behind them. It became a joke that has stayed with her until now.

Here at Vanessa's graduation, her staff and teachers tell stories like this to illustrate how much they've seen her grow. Not all the stories are funny, but the atmosphere remains joyfully poignant because we know, as much as it's possible to know, that Vanessa will leave here and be all right. She's gained sight of the kind of person she wants to be and stayed true to it through the setbacks. She's worked with the guidance given her, acknowledging her pain as part of her life and taking responsibility for the destructive ways she's responded to it in the past. In a poem she wrote titled "My Apology," Vanessa expresses a sense of genuine remorse that is rare among any teenagers, let alone those who have been badly hurt by the adults in their lives:

Knowing how I have hurt you
Makes me want to cry
Want to be alone in my room
Never look you in the eye.

And in another poem, "Perpetrator," Vanessa writes about how she has integrated her part of her emotional pain, a necessary step for healing:

Of course it hurts bad
Thoughts of you make me mad
But I have accepted it
I know I can't change it
I'm glad it was me
Because I'm the best person I can be!

The principal is talking now, telling about working with Vanessa in the school's production of *West Side Story* last year. His balding head, moustache, and big glasses made him a perfect Doc the Shopkeeper. Vanessa played Anita, Maria's best friend. She always sang along to the radio quite well before *West Side Story*, but this was her first performance in front of a real audience. She never quite shook her nervousness, but she did great in spite of it. The spirited defiance in the lines from the "America" song came alive when she sang them: "I love the isle of . . . Manhattan, / Smoke on your pipe and put . . . that in!"

The principal is winding up, and I look at Vanessa, glowing in her nervous-excited way. It's easy to see why the girls she's lived with admire her, beautiful as she is without drawing attention to it, without imitating some diva or provoking jealousy or comparison. You can also tell why the younger girls at this treatment center, the twelve- and thirteen-year-olds, look up to her and turn to her as if she were an older sister. She's figured out who she is; she's not trying to be someone else, and since she doesn't have to worry so much about herself, she's been able to care for them genuinely when they're in tears about trouble at home or with other kids on the unit.

I realize that I've made it sound as if Vanessa hasn't struggled much while she's been here. Well, it's somewhat true: when I started working as the weekend counselor on the unit she was assigned to, she had been here for almost six months and was already one of the leaders. I helped her with some of her homework and taught her how to kick a soccer ball with no spin on it, but we never really talked because she didn't need to. There's a temptation to call teenagers like Vanessa "good kids," but after a while I learned that the label is unfair. It shows that you see only what you want to see about them, disregarding everything they've done that has landed them in a treatment center. They may not like staff calling them on their bad behaviors, but they like being ignored even less. The whole truth about Vanessa is that she's a wonderful person because she has chosen—and still must choose—to act on the good inside her and not on the hatred and anger. Just as the pain will always be a part of her life, those emotionally destructive tendencies are still there, too. In a poem called "My Monster," she explains,

> *What happened to her you ask?*
> *I thought all of that was in the past*
> *Well obviously you thought wrong*
> *It has been a part of me all along.*

The only reason I've gotten to know Vanessa well is because, a few months ago, she slipped up. While on a home visit, she broke the coed rules of her program and then lied about it to her mom and her unit manager at Heritage. But she couldn't live with her conscience for long and confessed. When she came back from her visit, she basically had to earn all her trust and privileges back. It was a shock to the girls there to see her level dropped from a 5, the highest, to a 2, and it was embarrassing for Vanessa, but she accepted the consequence and started over, learning how to pay attention to her own needs and warning signs more.

And so, for the first time since I've worked here, Vanessa and I began to talk. She already had strong relationships with the female staff, but until then, she had been rightfully wary of male staff. Perhaps she recognized it as something she would need to overcome eventually. Some lines from another of Vanessa's poems, "In the Moment," capture what it's like to feel trapped to behave a certain way because you're afraid to act differently:

I am a fish in its bowl
Try to understand I'm not fake.
I feel like a character
In a drama play.

Vanessa told me sad stories about the violence at home and the anger towards her dad that she still felt so strongly. One of the great things we've been able to do together is read S. E. Hinton's book *The Outsiders*. I chose it because it's similar to *West Side Story*, and because it echoes Robert Frost when Pony Boy, one of the characters, is told to "stay gold." And for the last couple of months, my wife has become her volunteer mentor, meeting with her on campus once a week so that the two of them can talk for an hour.

Finally, Vanessa stands at the podium. She has received her diploma and is thanking her staff, teachers, and most of all, her mom and sister. After the luncheon, she'll leave campus with them and return to her world for good. There will still be moments when she feels pressured to put on an act and play along, but there have been many moments where she's chosen to step back from the situation and be herself. Without it having been said, all of us in that chapel know this about Vanessa, and while we'll miss her, we're smiling at each other, happy to see her go.

❉ ❉ ❉ ❉

It's been over a year since Vanessa graduated. Soon afterward, my wife and I moved out of the area and are now living abroad. We stay in contact, and Vanessa has told us about her triumphs and challenges in soccer, college, and the rest of life. Overall, she's successful because she keeps moving forward through both good and bad outcomes. In her most recent letter, she talked about how much she likes massage therapy school and what her goals are for graduation and beyond. And at the end, as with every e-mail and letter we send to each other, are the words "Stay Gold."

A Student to Remember

By Jacqueline Seewald

*T*had just started back in teaching after a long hiatus for child-raising and was feeling rather discouraged. Three out of my five classes were senior groups of special education students. These included learning disabled, emotionally disturbed, and physically handicapped. They had been all grouped together.

I was trained to teach English at the high school level, but had no special education credentials and felt completely out of my depth. The job was not what I had signed on for, nor did I feel equipped to handle it suitably. Some of my students were actually violent and disruptive in the classroom. I also found myself working with a supervisor who was difficult and unhelpful at best. I was seriously thinking about quitting.

In my homeroom was a quiet, red-headed boy who wore glasses. He was named "Bobby" and he was confined to a wheelchair. Bobby always had a smile for me. His manner was helpful and respectful. Needless to say, he was one of my favorite students. I knew little about Bobby's personal life or disability until my husband and I took our older son, Andy, to a 5K race one day. There was Bobby, ready to "run" in the wheelchair competition. We met his family there as well. They were wonderfully supportive people.

Bobby was very kind to our son, encouraging and positive. Bobby won his race, just as our son, Andrew, won in his own age competition. We went hoarse cheering for both boys. There were tears in my eyes as I watched each boy cross the finish line with the theme from "Chariots of Fire" playing in the background.

"Bobby's a wonderful kid," I told his father. "I wish all my students were like him."

"My wife and I completely agree with you," he replied.

"Has Bobby been in a wheelchair since birth?" my husband asked.

Bobby's father shook his head. "No, Bobby was paralyzed in an accident some years ago. Before that, he was a typical, energetic, athletic kid. But he's handled it well. Instead of feeling sorry for himself, Bobby's found ways to be successful in life. He's an excellent student and he's going to graduate with honors. He also finds ways to continue being an athlete—like today."

Later, I personally congratulated Bobby. "I admire your achievement. You were terrific."

Bobby actually blushed. "I just did my best." He shrugged. "I figure a person should always give everything their best effort."

Bobby's constructive, sunny view of life is something I've never forgotten. Bobby's courage and character were an inspiration to a lot of other students. He was extremely popular. I found his attitude inspiring as well. So I stayed at my job, giving my students my best efforts. Eventually, I went back to school. In graduate school, I improved my knowledge and abilities, becoming a much better teacher. Hopefully, I went on to inspire many of my students the way Bobby inspired me.

It's All Inside

By Josh Cox

*Y*ou are the first sub Philip has ever got along with."

One of the students is telling me this as I load the VCR with the *Toy Story* tape. They tell me their regular teacher never allows them to watch it.

"And I'm like, c'mon Mrs. Allen, it's not like *Toy Story* is *Faces of Death*, you know."

Earlier, outside at the track meet, Philip and his buddy Braulio were sitting at the only table on the field. Foothills from a Bob Ross painting filled the perimeter, while the sky above rivaled that of Montana—expansive and grand. Braulio challenged me to an arm wrestling match. We clasped hands and struggled. I won. Philip moved one chair closer, cracked his knuckles, and grinned.

"Sure," I say, stretching my fingers, "get me while I'm worn out."

"I am not gonna hurt you, Mr. Cox."

Philip put up a fight but I wouldn't let my knuckles touch the table.

Two girls from Mrs. Allen's class came over. Philip forgot about the arm wrestling. He started to talk about his achievements.

"Today," he told the two girls, "I threw the softball further than anyone else." Fifteen minutes later, he did the exact same thing with the shot put.

A couple of fourth graders came over to the table, trying to act courageous around their fifth-grade elders. Marco from Mrs. Allen's class scared them away, then turned to me and said, "Philip's going to districts."

"Marco, duh," said one of the girls. "Philip flunked two grades."

"Philip's twelve years old," the other girl said to me, all matter-of-fact.

They were saying all of this while he was right there in their company. I looked over at Philip, sitting at the end of the bench. His eyes bored holes through the table.

"I was held back one year," he said through gritted teeth.

No one said anything for a while. We sat and studied the panorama, the mesas, the way the morning light hit the clouds in Arizona. They never look the same by afternoon.

"Corazon got third in shot put," Braulio said.

Philip's face shot up.

"Oh yeah, but who got first, huh, Braulio?" We didn't know if Philip wanted to fight or play the braggart. "Who got first in the shot put, Braulio? Who got twenty-nine point six?"

Philip pounded the table with his fists, took a deep breath, and looked up at us with a smile wider than the football field.

"That's even better than I did last year."

"So," I said, "where do you guys go next year? For middle school. Is it Castle Dome?"

"Castle Dome," Philip nodded. "And if we make it to high school without dropping out, we all end up as Criminals."

"Criminals?" I asked.

"Yeah," said Philip. "That's the mascot of the high school. You might think you're looking at a bunch of future workers when you look at us, Mr. Cox. Future doctor. Future nurse. Future teacher. Not us. We're just a bunch of future Criminals. What was your mascot, Mr. Cox?"

I had to think about it for a minute.

"We were the Martians."

"The Martians?" All the kids began to laugh very hard. "That's retarded."

"I know," I said. "It's supposed to be for Mars, you know, the Roman God of War, but who's gonna think that, right? People hear the word *Martian* and what do they think? They just see the green guy with the big head on Looney Tunes. So that's my mascot story. But I don't get it. Why do they call you guys the Criminals?"

"It's 'cause we got that prison, that Territorial Prison. It's kind of like our claim to fame. If Yuma has a tourist trap, that's it. A hundred years ago, they locked up people there but they don't do it anymore. It's closed down. A state park."

"Hey Philip," said one of the girls, "Wasn't your dad a prisoner there?"

"Ha ha," said Philip. "The prison shut down in 1909."

"Oh, okay. Then it was your grandpa, right?"

"Just shut up, Tara. But, yeah, high school, I might not even make it that far. I might be out of here. Might be going to Salinas, California." He got up off the bench. "It's too hot here!" he yelled, as he jogged away, clutching his two blue ribbons for an impromptu victory lap around the football field.

"Well then you'll be too cold there!" Tara called after him. In no time, both she and her cohort, future cheerleaders, broke into a sing-song cadence.

"Philip in Salinas / He's gonna freeze his—" I sounded the air horn before the girls got to the rhyme.

On cue, everyone began to scramble indoors.

Back in Mrs. Allen's classroom, the kids were beside themselves with excitement. Jubilant after claiming school-wide victory on the tug of war and hyper from a morning's worth of sugar, the kids in Mrs. Allen's room would not listen to the video on phyla, but, with a little help from Philip, I handed them their ribbons.

"Philip never helps out Mrs. Allen," one of the girls told me.

"He doesn't help the other subs, either," Braulio said.

"Maybe if they were like Mr. Cox, I would," Philip said from the back of the room, where he was handing out 100-yard dash ribbons.

"You might be surprised, Philip," I said. "A lot more people out there are like me than you might think. We're not all future criminals, no matter where the prison is."

He edged closer, handing out softball-throw ribbons now. "What do you mean?"

His demeanor was diffident, but I could tell that I had his attention.

"If it exists at all, the prison," I said, "really isn't outside of you. For most of us, it's inside of us, Philip. If you let other people tell you what you are, then they define you. There's a lot of power in that."

Philip stopped pretending as if he were only half-listening. I had his complete attention.

"It doesn't matter where you go if you're like that. If the prison's in you, you'll be a criminal in Salinas as much as here in Yuma."

"And if it isn't?"

"If it isn't," I said, "then you'll be truly free."

He didn't talk after that, just went about handing out the rest of the ribbons. But I could tell that I'd given him something to think about. He was obviously a deep thinker. How the kid managed to get held back was beyond me. Maybe that's why I was always a substitute, and never a "regular" teacher.

Later, after I'd dismissed the class for the day and the classroom had cleared out, Philip hung behind the others. When it was just the two of us in the room, he walked over to the teacher's desk, and placed something on it.

I was on the other side of the room, erasing the board, and didn't see what it was. Philip hurried from the room, shouting, "See you later, Mr. Cox!" over his shoulder.

I walked over to the desk and saw what he'd left for me.

It was one of his blue ribbons. He had placed a piece of notebook paper underneath it. He had written on it: "If a prison can be inside you, I guess being a winner can be too. I've already got one of these, so this is yours. Thanks Mr. Cox."

I never saw Philip again. Criminal or doctor, loser or winner, I guess he could have gone either way. I know which one I think he is.

Empty Hand, Empty Mind

By Domenico Capilongo

I can still remember the first day I met Anna. I entered the classroom in my pure white karate uniform, black belt, and the Buddhist monk slippers that I bought when I lived in Japan. The students turned to face me and I could feel them take a slight breath in. "Has he come to teach us or kill us?" Anna said, scanning the room to see if she could get a laugh. I smiled. My fellow teachers, when they found out what I was teaching, asked, "Are you going to teach karate to the alt. ed. kids? Are you sure that's what they need?" I soon discovered that it was exactly what they needed, especially Anna.

Teaching alternative education has been one of the most fulfilling experiences I have had in my career. It's been almost a decade and I still get excited about working with these kids. They are a unique bunch of teens, ranging in age from sixteen to nineteen, who have struggled unsuccessfully with so many personal problems that the regular school system simply has no place for them.

Sometimes they tend to be rude and rough around the edges, hardened by a tough life. They're not quick to trust but often they are so honest and caring that they're even funny about it. Once they get to know that you believe in them, they give you a deep level of respect.

"So, sir, are we gonna fight?" Anna said, flicking her dark hair and chewing her gum vigorously.

"Yes, we are going to spar but that's not what karate's about. Does anyone here know what the word karate means?"

Silence.

"Well, it means 'empty hand,' but not just because we don't use weapons. It's also because some people believe that if you practice really hard, you can attain a level of calm and inner peace. A kind of emptiness where everything is fine and nothing bothers you."

"Okay, the first step is to see what kind of shape you are all in." Every two weeks I put the class through a rigorous fitness test during which, among other things, they have to perform as many perfect push-ups as possible.

"But sir, are you serious? I'm a girl. I can't do push-ups." It always amazes me how every young woman who takes my nine-week course starts out being able to do only a few push-ups and ends up in double digits. Anna was no exception. I think she managed to surprise herself the most.

It's through this physical training that I get the students to improve their self-esteem. Intense warm-ups and one hour of yoga per week helps them breathe, stretch, and feel comfortable with their bodies. Although these students are in their teens they haven't exercised in a very long time. Two weeks into the course, in the middle of stretching, Anna yelled out, "I haven't been able to touch my toes in years!"

One morning, Anna arrived early. She pulled me to the side of the classroom and said, "Sir, I was taking a shower last night and felt muscles I never thought I had. I feel great. Look, feel my arm. It's bigger than my brother's!"

One of the most integral parts of karate, often called its soul, is the practice of "kata" or "forms." The practitioner moves in a set pattern, defending against an imaginary opponent. It requires a certain level of confidence and memorization.

I loved teaching the first simple pattern to Anna. She really believed she was stupid and that there was no way she could memorize anything. It was wonderful to watch the slow change in her begin. After a few lessons she started jumping up and down. "Sir, I got it. I practiced at home and now I can do it." She felt as though she could do anything.

One of karate's most famous masters has said that the true aim of karate is the perfection of character. The hardest part of teaching character comes when I give a lesson on how to avoid a fight. This was very difficult for Anna to understand, and possibly for all teens, who are so full of a false sense of pride that if someone looks at them wrong they take it as a sign of disrespect.

"Through the practice of karate," I told her, "you can feel good about your body and yourself. You can learn to be confident and not let anything or anyone faze you. Empty your mind of any anger or fear."

Anna had struggled in the past with anger and had gotten into several street fights. Near the end of the course, she rushed into the classroom red-faced after lunch, surrounded by a group of her peers. "It worked, sir. It really worked. I went to the cafeteria, this bitch was staring me down, and she said something. I know what she said. She called me a 'ho.' I stopped and I took a deep breath, just like you said, and I could feel it just going away. Last year I would have killed her, you know? But I didn't. I just cleared my mind and walked past her. You were right."

I end the nine weeks with sparring—for most, the highlight of the course. At this point, all the students have come a long way, both mentally and physically, yet I could see that part of Anna still resisted the whole philosophy of karate.

After sparring with their classmates in a safe and controlled manner, each student gets to fight me. They're all usually quite tame and relaxed but Anna decided this was her chance to get me.

We bowed, but I noticed she just nodded—a foreshadowing of her true intentions. I put up my guard. She crunched her fists close to her, as though she was hiding something, and backed herself into a corner. She locked eyes with me and then, like a championship cricket bowler, she ran towards me and swung her arm high over her head, sweeping down to my face. At the last moment I moved out of the way and tapped her shoulder lightly with my finger. She caught herself, backed away, and tried again. After four attempts she was breathing quite heavily. I ended the match and when we did our final bow, she gave me the faintest little grin that suggested that maybe, just maybe, she understood what I was trying to teach her.

Sammi's Priceless Popsicle Stick

By Cristy Trandahl

"My dad bought this new deluxe model train set for me on his last business trip to Tokyo. That's in Japan," eight-year-old Brett began. "The engine has a super speed accelerator and real working lights. But because this cost tons of money, my mom says it's for display, not play, so I can't pass it around. You might disconnect a car or something." The little boy smiled smugly at his classmates.

I yawned. Rolled my eyes toward the ceiling. Sighed.

"Thank you, Brett. That was another fascinating toy from around the globe. Does anyone have Show and Share questions for Brett about his deluxe model train?" My eyes scanned the eager faces of my second-grade students.

A chubby hand shot up.

"Timmy?"

"How much did it cost?" Timmy inquired.

"Triple digits!" boasted Brett. His face glowed as the class gasped in unison at the staggering cost of his display-not-play-toy.

I butted in. "Did anyone else bring something for Show and Share?"

Of course, I already knew the answer. Three students clutched items in their little arms, eager to brag up their booty. Liz held out a computer game, the latest handheld phenomenon. Joey waved a two-foot-long remote control speedboat in the air. Lindsey stuck a video cassette tape labeled "Family Vacation to Europe, 1990" in my face.

"Me! Me! Me!" The students clucked like hungry chickens.

Again I sighed audibly.

It was my first year teaching second grade. My first month of school, and already I was bored stiff by—of all things—Show and Share! Week after week the same few students paraded into the room on Fridays toting the latest trendy toy or fashionable clothing accessory. Maybe a story about how much money their grandparents spent on a pair of tennis shoes for them. Vacations. Snowmobiles. Savings Bonds.

And week after week, the rest of the students sat hunched, sagging with envy or greed or despair, wishing that they had merchandise others would gloat over. For some of the students in our middle-class public school, a trip to Disneyland may as well be a trip to the moon. And for these children, owning a new remote control car was as unlikely as their parents owning a new vehicle themselves.

The disparity between economic levels of the students in my class was most evident during Show and Share. And it was dividing us all. There had to be a better way.

"Students, let's move on to mathematics now," I suggested. I decided that during lunch break I would ask more seasoned teachers for advice on how I could turn "Brag and Boast" day into genuine sharing time.

An experienced teacher, Donna advised me: "Encourage the students to bring in stories or items that tell about themselves. Things that they've made. Nothing brand new or expensive. Personal items that tell about their lives." Thank goodness for knowledgeable mentors.

Before dismissal that afternoon, I stood before my second-grade class and explained the new Show and Share rules. The kids just couldn't get it.

"Nothing expensive?" Brett shot out of his seat, mouth agape. "What else is there?"

Joey was appalled. "No new toys?"

"How 'bout cash?" Liz offered.

"Nope. Nope. Nope," I shook my head. "Let's get creative! See you tomorrow, class. Remember, next Friday is Show and Share. I can't wait to see what amazing ideas you come up with."

The next Friday, after roll-call, lunch money, announcements, and the Pledge of Allegiance, I eagerly invited students to sit in the familiar Show and Share circle. No packages rattled. No shopping bags shook.

"Who wants to share first today?" I surveyed the room for hands.

"Brett?" The usually talkative boy merely stared at me.

"Liz?" Like talking to a brick wall.

"Joey?" Ditto.

My shoulders slumped. "Didn't anyone bring something for Show and Share today?"

Liz stood up, the spokesperson for the class. "Teacher, we don't get it. If we can't bring in cool stuff, expensive stuff, we can't think of nothing else."

"Anything else," I corrected her. "Yes, I understand that this may be difficult. But the world is so diverse, so beautiful, so . . . " I could have cried. My first month of teaching and I couldn't even teach Show and Share. "There's more to life than the mall, that's all."

Silence filled the classroom like quick dry cement pouring into a hole. No one fidgeted. No feet shuffled. No whispering or talking or laughing. Only the tick-tick-tick of the electric wall clock. And twenty pairs of little eyes staring at me.

"No one?" I pleaded one last time.

Just then Sammi stood up, slowly like someone was lifting her.

"I do, teacher," Sammi's little voice creaked like a desk top's hinges when someone opened it. Sammi was shy. Painfully shy.

"Sammi, please. Share with us." It made me nervous just to watch this little girl, all freckled and redheaded and pale, stand before the class.

"I . . . I brought this," Sammi began in a whisper, holding out a stick for us to see. As she spoke, her voice became clearer and more confident. "It's a Popsicle stick. See? A cherry one." Red dye still stained the stick. "And it was for me last week. I was sick last week, remember teacher? I had a fever and my throat really hurt. My mom was sick, too, real sick. But she knew I needed to get better. So mom drove to the grocery store in the middle of the night even though she was tired and fevery, and she got me Popsicles—a whole box—banana, and root beer, and cherry, my favorite. And in the night I got to eat one and it made my throat feel better. And now I'm better and I'm back at school." Sammi smiled, revealing a missing front tooth. She shifted her weight on her worn pink sneakers, and stuffed the Popsicle stick in the front pocket of her faded jeans.

"So now I'm all better," she added. "And I . . . I just wanted to show everybody what my mom did for me, how much she loves me . . ."

Sammi sat.

The students smiled.

I swallowed hard, choking back tears at Sammi's miraculously simple story. "Thank you, Sammi. That . . . that is some Popsicle stick. And your mom . . . your mom must really, really love you."

Composing myself, I smoothed my skirt and took another deep breath, afraid I would break down in front of my students. After a minute, I continued, "And that, class, is what sharing is about. That was the most valuable Show and Share lesson we've seen yet. Sammi's priceless Popsicle stick."

She Gently Opened Doors

By Lawrence D. Elliott

*T*eachers open the door, but you must enter by your-self." Thus it is written in an ancient Chinese proverb, but you would not have been able to convince me of the truth in that statement in the fall of 1973. Growing up as a black kid in San Diego, it was truly the first year I would be placed into what might be considered hostile territory and forced to confront issues that would be a part of my life into adulthood.

I had graduated from the sixth grade and it was time to start junior high school. At that time, most junior high schools started at grade seven and ended at grade nine. My mother decided she wanted me to go to Pershing Junior High School, located in a predominantly white area, because she felt I might be in a better learning atmosphere. Back then, walking through the doors of a school in the inner city and walking though the doors of a school in a more affluent area were truly like night and day. It was not something I looked forward to.

"I don't want to go to school there," I told her. "Those white people don't want me there and I don't want to be there."

Not looking up from the enrollment form, she continued to complete it. "You're going to have to learn to deal with different people," she said. "You might as well start while you're young, instead of waiting until you're my age." Her reaction made it clear that she wasn't telling me about my enrollment at Pershing in order to open a debate. She was telling me to allow me to prepare for the inevitable. The discussion was closed.

I wondered about my friends. How would I survive alone? My mind created a very ugly picture and I believed the summer was not going to be enjoyable. But as time passed, I discovered many of my friends' parents had the same idea and I wouldn't be alone after all. I was thrilled to discover that my best friend Henry would also be attending. We were like brothers and my mood began to change knowing I would have him by my side.

On the first day, we all gathered at the bus pick-up spot on the corner near Jerry's Market. Then, there it was. A bright yellow bus! Now they'll really see us coming, I thought. How could anyone miss a bright yellow bus in the Southern California sun?

As we arrived on that first day, we felt like exhibits in a museum. As each of us exited the bus, crowds gathered and stared in disbelief. We felt like we were invading their neighborhood instead of attending school. It was only the beginning.

There were the "usual" racial taunts. There were the fights. Sometimes, when you found yourself alone, groups would harass you and jump you. Most of the time, we would stay in groups and it would be a little better. We didn't take any physical abuse. Often, we wouldn't take any verbal abuse, either. We fought back! Most of the time we won the fights. But even when we won, we somehow felt we lost. School wasn't supposed to be like this.

Somehow, a test I had taken showed my learning ability was below normal. I was placed in a special English class. Now, it wasn't just some racist idiot trying to make me feel like less of a person. Now a test score showed that perhaps it was true, or so I thought. I walked into class that first day, eyes moistened by the hurt I felt, not wanting to talk to anyone. Then, she appeared. Ms. Davila, my teacher for the class.

She was rather young, thin, with a pleasant voice and demeanor. I wouldn't say she was drop-dead gorgeous, but over time she became the most beautiful teacher at school. Her greatest skill was her ability to teach while understanding how we each had very emotional feelings about being in her class. She also knew how hard it was for those of us who rode that yellow bus to adjust to being placed in this atmosphere and still try to learn. She was the perfect teacher, in the perfect place, at the perfect time. God answered my prayer before I'd had a chance to even bow my head over the matter.

The class size was small enough with ten students for her to give each of us the attention we needed. She spent a good amount of time with me. Early on, she had discovered I was a slow reader. She told me I didn't read like most people. I had very good comprehension, but I had the desire to read every sentence perfectly, so I would go back over sentences two or even three times. In a controlled testing atmosphere, it meant wasting valuable time. She worked with me on exercises to get my reading techniques corrected and by the end of the second year I had improved greatly. Even today, I'm not what you would call a speed-reader, but I am much better and it made me embrace reading much more. It was no longer a laborious chore.

After a couple of weeks, she assigned me to write an essay. The subject was simple—and *powerful*—in so many ways. I was to explain where I saw myself after completing her class. Now, even though you would assume it would be overwhelming for a kid in a remedial English class to write an essay, I really wasn't scared of the task. In sixth grade, one of my teachers had assigned us to write a short story. I wrote mine and included illustrations. Stick figures, really. Since then, I knew I could write well.

When Ms. Davila read my essay, she was impressed with my ability to put my ideas into a cohesive form at such a young age. Eventually, she made it my regular assignment to write at least one per week. Often, I would write more just for the love of it. Whether the subject was about family life of Native Americans or my family's roots from California to Louisiana, she would sit down with me, correct my errors, and suggest better ways of wording and structuring my thoughts. I really looked forward to her class every day. I could feel my previously sagging self-esteem lifted to new heights.

This led to her final important lesson. I'm not sure if she intended to make it part of her curriculum. One day, as I was sitting in the classroom between assignments, I noticed something about the class I hadn't noticed before. There were white kids, too! In fact, half of the class was white. Another thing I noticed is many of the kids at school were not calling me racial names and not picking fights with me. Oh, some were, but many weren't. They seemed to be kinder than the others. In fact, toward the end of the first year, we had what could be termed as a mini race riot. But not every kid felt the same way. I was shocked to hear one of the white kids saying how stupid a friend was who called a black girl an ugly racial name. "Where did all of these kids come from?" I asked myself. Were they new to the school? Or could Ms. Davila's kindness have allowed me to look past the imbeciles and spot decent people?

As I moved on to the tenth grade, I looked back and found I truly enjoyed my time at Pershing. The first year was the most difficult. There were problems later, but they didn't seem to be as hard to deal with as the ones I experienced during that first year.

Would I say this if I hadn't had Ms. Davila? I don't want to know the answer to that question. I thank God she was there and I hope every kid has a Ms. Davila to guide them through the rough spots. And there will be rough spots, that's for sure.

Often, I have wondered what happened to Ms. Davila. Did she ever marry? Did she have a family? How did her life turn out? I always hoped her life was as rewarding as was my experience with her. Once I tried to find her, but I was unsuccessful. But if she is reading these words, I would like to thank her for teaching me in more ways than she could imagine. I carried those lessons with me throughout my life and I have thought of her often.

I thought of her through my high school years every time I had to read something or write an essay or short story . . . and could do it! I thought of her while serving in the military with people of different cultures and backgrounds and how I learned to look past the bad apples for the nice shiny ones. Or when I had to train someone and that person felt awkward and unsure. I hope I was as effective with them as she was with me.

Sometimes, I think of her when I have a client who is a teacher and I am reviewing a real estate contract with them. Maybe it takes me back to that little classroom where a kid who felt his lowest was taught important lessons by a caring teacher who showed him how to take back his dignity. Is she a Ms. Davila?

There have been other people who have had a large impact on my life. But I can truly say that she came along at a point in my life when her presence was much needed and made an everlasting impression on my life. She gently opened doors and gave me the confidence to go through them by myself.

Music for Life

By Barbara W. Campbell

*T*he whole world needs a song in their hearts," Mom would say with a twinkle in her eye and her curls bouncing. "We'll cheer those around us by singing, if we sing well, and smile while doing it." Our family singing lessons were often spent laughing, sometimes crying, and always enjoying them without the television on. Although we don't sing together these days apart from Christmas, my brothers and sisters and I often reminisce about the great times we had under Mom's musical tutelage and the invaluable lessons we learned.

Today in my chosen career of teaching young children, I perceive that all children want to be recognized or to stand out for doing something well. It's my place to encourage them to try the things that seem hard. Even if perfection isn't reached on the first go, kindness and a smile give the child confidence to make another attempt. Success will come with a little persistence. Being happy and using good manners is easy to teach. It's straight out of Mom's instructions, "Show by example." I wished I had the patience Mom had.

The acoustics were good in the family room, and Mom lined us up in front of the piano: three boys and three girls aged between four and twelve. I was the middle child of the younger three. Mom started by teaching us to sing the musical scales. She played middle C on the piano and we sang, "do-re-mi-fa-so-la-ti-do," and down again. Every session began this way. Scales and more scales, we weren't allowed to jump right into learning a new song without completing our warm-ups of voice exercises. The bouncing one, where we sang, "do-re-do-mi-do-fa-do-so-do-la-do-ti-do-do," always sent a wave of laughter through us.

When Mom introduced a new song, she taught all of us the melody before adding the alto or bass parts. We needed to get the melody right first and then add the harmonies when we were able. That was pretty much her method of facing life as well. I learned that love, honesty, and unselfishness made up the essentials of a solid foundation for a happy and peaceful life.

The refrain, "Birds that can sing and won't sing, should be made to sing," represented an underpinning principle Mom grew up with and tried to instill in all of us. Our family name wasn't Partridge or Von Trapp, but we knew to try our best, reach those notes, pronounce those weird words, and leave off our pushing and shoving. Sometimes Mom had to enforce control with the yardstick, a flat wooden ruler she kept in the hall closet. My eldest brother, Mark, instigated hiding the yardstick so Mom couldn't find it. Of course, this delighted the rest of us as we lightheartedly teased her, knowing we had no choice but to eventually knuckle down and sing it right! Mom had lots of patience. She said, "Learning to sing properly is serious business and this ruler will drive foolishness out the door."

As a part of my singing family, it wasn't my outstanding talent or winning personality that gave me a sense of achievement. Singing my note correctly alongside my brothers and sisters gave me a place in the scheme of things, a sense of my own significance, and boosted my self-esteem. We surprised ourselves sounding so good. Sight-reading a sheet of music far surpassed learning to sing a tune along with the radio.

Singing at home was easy but to sing in front of other people made my heart pound wildly. On the other hand, how could we make people happy if we only sang in our family room? Yes, we accepted an invitation to sing. Standing, waiting to start, with strangers' blank faces staring back at you . . . Whew!

The first time was scary but then the applause sounded great. The smiles broke out on the audience's faces and they clapped as we sang. I remember thinking, "Maybe this isn't so bad after all." Of course, singing for the hard-of-hearing down at the Old Folks' Home was probably a good place to start. However, we kept at it, the crowds changed and the venues were different but the team spirit grew as our individual confidence increased. Now my siblings and I enjoy the rewards of this discipline Mom taught us around the piano. We learned firsthand that even those things that we enjoyed doing most of the time required occasional restraint and effort. If we are committed and persistent, the efforts reap great rewards. Obedience always appears to be more advantageous in retrospect than breaking the rules. My brothers, sisters, and I still enjoy music in some form or another and we're committed to teaching our own children the joys and sometimes hard work of learning music.

Today, cassette tapes or compact discs offer the student an easier way to learn to sing or play an instrument. Pianos are not always available. A group of children sit on the floor clapping to a new song. I turn the volume up. I see they feel the rhythm as they keep perfect time. We listen first, and then we sing along. The children fall over laughing while attempting a round. Everyone ends up singing the same line.

"That is funny," I say. "Jacob, you're singing the loudest, and that's causing everyone to join you on your line." I tell them, "It's okay. We'll try again. Practice and more practice will work. All the boys sing 'Row row row your boat' with Jake and then the girls follow me, and start 'Row row row your boat,' while the boys sing 'Gently down the stream.'" It seems the children would rather laugh at themselves than get it right. Remembering a recording I had, I asked the children to sit quietly while I found it and put it into the cassette player. When the tape played the round the children said, "We can sing it now that we heard how it is supposed to go." That they did with much pride in themselves. Perhaps we only learn happy tunes, but the children are more contented and less quarrelsome seeing for themselves that it sounded better when done correctly. My confidence and teaching skills must be attributed to Mom's insistence that we learned to sing and sing well. After all, as she said, "Anything worth doing is worth doing right." Mom could threaten her own children with the yardstick, but teaching other people's children is a different thing. Offering a reward works for good behavior and singing or playing more scales helps the mischievous ones pay attention. The melodies of life such as speaking kindly, using good manners, respecting elders, sharing, and forgiving when wronged could never be replaced with harmonies like wealth, success, or beauty and produce beautiful music or a citizen with integrity. I now understand the lessons Mom taught us were bigger and more important than music and a simple melody.

His Story

By Tab Lloyd

I love to read to my class. As a teacher, I know that literature helps all students learn. But for those with special needs, there is a spark that comes when they connect to a character in a book, especially when connecting with peers or family members is not always easy.

One of the storytellers in my room is Robert Munsch, the author of *Love You Forever*. Oh, he's written quite a bit more than that, and each book gets a fair amount of class time, but *Love You Forever* is definitely at the top of our "best book" list.

So each day, we find ourselves plopped down on the reading rug or outside under a tree reading a stack of books, and *Love You Forever* is always included.

We laugh at the boy's antics throughout his growth stages, and scream with the annoyed mother. But despite the mother's frustration at her son's misbehavior, she always finds the time to rock him and sing of her unconditional love for him.

Most students in my class seem to enjoy the story on some level. One girl, Lottie, is a small fourth grader with Down syndrome. She scrambles into my lap as we read and sing along with the mother's love song. Charlie, who has cerebral palsy, is in fifth grade and is too "grown up" to participate physically, but still enjoys the connection he has with the book. The others take part in various ways, but sadly, one student seems to have no connection at all.

This student is Sameer. His eyes gaze into the lights or off into the sky as this story and others are read day after day. He clasps his hands in front of his eyes and squeezes vigorously and repeatedly from his elbows, staring at the movement he creates. Rocking back and forth, he hums at a pitch that would get any dog's attention. He's quite busy; however, his mind is distant. I am not sure about the connections he makes with the world around him. I wonder if he is even listening or understanding at all.

Sameer has autism.

I had never worked with a child with autism before this year; it has been a challenge. But we move on daily—working, singing, and reading—hoping that one day a connection will be made.

"Mrs. Lloyd, it's 1:30—time to read," a student reminds me one Friday afternoon.

Looking at Sameer, I ask, "Outside or inside?" with my voice as well as my hands.

No answer.

I ask again, "Out or in?"

"Out, in," he repeats.

"Well, which is it?" His hands move up and down alternately as he mimics my sign for "which one?"

"Out or in?"

"In," he says with his finger pointing at the floor.

"In it is! To the rug!" I don't know whether he really wants to stay in, or if he's just repeating the last thing I said again.

As the students sit around the rug, Sameer stands, rocking, with his hands clasped in front of him.

"What do you need, Sameer?" He stops rocking at the sound of his name.

"Need," he repeats. His eyes look at me. I know what he needs. I just want him to tell me. I want to hear the words:

"I need a chair, Mrs. Lloyd. My legs don't cross as easily as those of the other students, and I'm uncomfortable with sitting so long, even though I like the stories."

That's what I want to hear, but today, it doesn't come. Honestly, I'm not sure that he would say it if he could articulate himself well. I don't know that he enjoys the stories. I don't know if he understands that the stories are about people like him, who experience love, friendship, happiness, or frustration. Maybe the classroom routine is such a part of him that he listens to stories just because it's time to do so.

I give up on getting the response I want. The other students are restless and ready for the stories.

"Do you need a chair?"

"Yes," Sameer signs and speaks—just like me.

With Sameer in his chair, the students choose *Love You Forever*, as always. Lottie happily jumps up on my lap and joins me in singing the mother's song. We sing together, and then she hops back down to her spot on the rug. Each time we come to the song, a different student asks for a turn to rock with me. After the fourth chorus, I look out at the group, wondering who will ask next.

Sameer catches my eye. He's not rocking, not squeezing his hands together, not humming. He's looking at me—very intently, and straight into my eyes.

"Do you want a turn?"

"Yes," he tells me, without hesitation.

"Come on then."

Sameer lifts himself out of his chair, gingerly steps around the fingers and feet on the rug, and slowly weights himself on the rocking chair, with me sandwiched between them. He seems uncomfortable, but not necessarily that he is sitting on me, but more so that the chair doesn't feel like it's supposed to.

Being almost as big as I am, Sameer is quite heavy and awkward to sit with, but we rock back and forth while the class sings the song. When we finish, Sameer looks at the book.

He points to the boy, and says, "Bay."

"Yes, Sameer, that's the baby."

Pointing to the mother, he says, "Ma."

"And that's Mom. You're right!"

Just then, as unexpected tears pool in my eyes, his mom walks in the door. I had forgotten that she was picking him up for a dental appointment. The sight of Sameer on my lap, on top of the rocking chair was too much for her to keep in. She immediately starts to laugh as I wipe my eyes.

"What are you doing on Mrs. Lloyd?"

"Reading a book, Mom," I tell her, starting to giggle myself.

Sameer points to the mother in the book again.

"Ma."

He then points to his mom.

"Ma."

"That's her, Sameer—that's your mom!"

He points to the boy, and then to himself.

"Bay."

"And you are her baby."

Sameer's mother stops laughing, and my tears keep rolling.

"What did he say?"

"Tell her again, Sameer."

Again, he points and says, "Ma," and then "bay" as if he had done it a million times before.

Sameer starts to rock, moving the chair by his force. When the momentum hits him just right, he rises, facing his mom. Speechless from shock, she cradles his face in her hands, and starts to laugh again. It's not the same as before; this time her laughter is sprinkled with tears. Sameer's arms reach out, and he extends his body into the shape of a "T," and then leans his head into her shoulder. She echoes his movements, and they share an embrace.

I look at my students as they stare in amazement. Even they can see the spark Sameer has shared with us. The connection he has made from the classroom story to his very own life helps us all grow a little on this very day.

Bigger Than Mt. Rainier

By Lancer Kind

*F*or me, a typical winter week went like this: work in a cubicle forty hours Monday through Friday, on Friday night question my sanity about what time I was going to get up, then Saturday morning get up before there was light in the sky, and while the rest of Seattle slept beneath rain clouds, drive two hours to a local ski area to teach snowboarding. All for pay that would just cover food and gas.

Is this the right way to recharge during a weekend?

Sure it was hard getting up at 5:30 a.m. But every time I arrived at the ski area something interesting happened. Perhaps it was the mountain air; maybe it was the great students; hell, maybe it was the challenge of the bad ones— but no matter how tired I was when I arrived, by the time

I walked the half mile from employee parking to the class assembly area, I was excited.

One such spring morning at Crystal Mountain, the sun peeked over the mountains and made the snow, those frozen crystals of water, shine brighter than diamonds.

"It's a goggle-tan day," I said as my class assembled from either the parking lot or from catching an early run down the mountain. My students were Zak, Haley, Zak (yes, there were two Zaks), and Adam who was eight. Haley was sixteen, Zak and Zak were nine and eleven respectively. Zak and Zak were throwing snowballs at each other as they did every morning.

Haley said, "I can't believe they're still doing that."

One Zak had his snowboard stuck in the ground so its tip pointed in the air. He huddled behind it until the other Zak's barrage wore thin, and then he returned fire.

"This is the last day of class, after all. Perhaps it's because they have the same name. Only one Zak may leave the ski area . . . alive."

Adam sat next to Haley out of the line of fire. He was the quiet one in the class, the "still waters run deep" kid. "Maybe they're just dumb," he said.

Both Zaks heard this and for the next thirty seconds, they put all their might into snowball production and air-borne delivery in our direction. Haley suffered collateral damage and retreated. After a snowball clocked me in the helmet, things had to settle down. I negotiated a cease fire after a few retaliatory snowball strikes on each Zak.

"You're going to miss us," Haley said.

"Yes, I—"

Kyle, my supervisor, walked up with a kid from someone else's class.

"Travis's class left early. Can you take him until you see his class?"

"Sure," I said. I'd seen the other class and knew he would be able to keep up with us.

I didn't catch exactly when the trouble started, or how it happened. One minute my students were waiting for the clock to tick to starting time, talking and enjoying the spring sun, and the next minute, Adam told Travis to shut up but Travis kept laughing. It was kind of a mean laugh. Adam stood up and pointed at Travis. "You don't laugh at me. I don't like you."

"Hey, take it easy. It's time to go," I said. I attached my front foot onto my snowboard then used my back leg to kick against the snow and scoot myself forward like a skate boarder. Adam was already ahead of me, the rest of the class scooted behind us.

"I'm not riding up with that kid," Adam said.

The lift chairs hold six people, which meant we were supposed to use only one because people waiting in line like to see things running without delay. But Adam looked serious. "Alright," I said. "But you ride up with me."

Haley, Adam, and I rode one chair, the Zaks and Travis rode the chair behind us. On the ride up I tried to get him to talk. "So what's going on?"

"He made fun of my snowboard."

"I think he was just making a joke."

"He shouldn't laugh at me and I hate him."

Adam didn't want to talk about it anymore. Never before had I had a student say that about another kid. We unloaded midway up the mountain. I kept the two separated as much as possible and started the lesson on how to ride on a steep and uneven terrain.

"Remember how we did this last week? Keep your shoulders level with the snowboard. The goal is to make smooth right then left turns so the track left in the snow mimics a snake slithering down the mountain. Each of you rides until you reach the bottom of this pitch. I'll go last and give feedback."

Haley, the Zaks, and then Travis slid down the slope. Each of them started on the left edge of the snowboard leaving a C-shaped track in the snow, then they switched to the right edge which made the snowboard carve a "backwards C" to the right, then left, and right, and so on until the tracks they left behind were shaped like S's in a continuous pattern, like snakes had wiggled down the mountain.

As Adam came down, he easily made the left turn that created the C, but when he wanted to go right, his legs stayed straight and stiff, and the snowboard wobbled out of balance. He retreated to his left edge and skidded on it down to where the rest of the class waited. The racket the board made shaving the top layer of snow was like gritty fingernails scraping a chalkboard.

Adam could do better. The previous week he'd made S-turns so smooth you would have thought his snowboard was made from snakeskin. Obviously he was upset, and it was having an effect on his boarding.

Class continued down the mountain. I worked with each person on their technique and by the time we reached the bottom everyone was riding better than they had the previous week. Everyone, that is, except for Adam. His snowboard still shaved the ice like a rusty razor. Whatever was bothering him wasn't going away. On the next lift ride, I arranged it so just Adam and I rode one chair, the rest of the class on the other.

"Adam, I know you can ride that run better."

"That kid makes me so mad."

I wasn't sure what to say, so I changed the subject, and we talked about what he was doing in school and home. He'd always been a brooder, but I'd never seen him this angry.

We rode further on a second lift that took the class all the way to the peak. We met Travis's class at the top, and I gladly transferred Travis to it. My class took a short hike to look at our neighbor, Mt. Rainier. The scale of the volcano's glaciers and chasms made everything else small and temporary. If anything could give someone a new perspective, it would be Mt. Rainier.

Adam was quiet. Zak was talking to the other Zak about the possibility of sledding down the volcano.

Haley said, "You're crazy. You'd fall into a crevasse and die."

The other Zak started talking about how they could save themselves with ropes.

"Let's ride," I said and we went down the slope. Adam still struggled. Halfway down the pitch he did his best to shift the snowboard onto its other edge, but his legs were stiff like he was angry at gravity and he fell. Instead of getting up, he just sat and punched at the snow. I stopped next to him and waved the class to go on to the bottom of the pitch.

"You're having a tough day. What's wrong?"

"I don't know!" he said and stared at the snow.

Since Travis wasn't anywhere near us, I was stumped. Adam's helmet was silver, and red goggles stretched across his eyes. I could hardly see his face at all because his head hung down as if he watched something in the snow crystals that covered the slope. My reflection in his helmet watched me, and I watched Adam and waited because he was working something out. It was as if the reflection was an indicator that though he wasn't looking at me, I floated in his thoughts as some kind of observer. But reflections don't have a voice, so I gave it one: "Hey man.

I'm really trying here. What can I do to help you have a good time?"

"I don't know," he said and stopped reading the snow. Whatever he saw in the crystals, he kept secret but his eyes said, wow, this guy really cares.

I patted him on the shoulder. "Shall we catch up with the class?"

He nodded and stood up. "My mom's got a new boyfriend." Though he looked at our class below, he didn't leave.

"Is his name Travis?"

"No. I hate being friends with a stranger just because she likes him. And he makes these stupid jokes all the time."

After a moment I said, "How many snowboard instructors does it take to change a light bulb?"

Adam grinned and said, "I'm not taking this!"

I expected him to continue down by shaving the snowboard's left edge over the slope and leaving behind a trail of abraded ice crystals. Instead, the board slipped into each turn guided by his relaxed legs. Left turn, right turn, left turn, then right, tracing an S into the snow. It was the spirit of the snake, and it had slithered its way into his snowboard's core.

When we reached the rest of the class, Haley said, "You'll never guess what. We just found out that Zak and Zak are related!"

Adam said, "You guys are kidding!"

The Zaks explained how they were related to each other through some tangle of cousins and aunts that no one could follow.

Finally Adam interrupted them, "Let's go ride!"

Class continued: mountains, fresh air, blue sky, and now everyone making S-turns. I was reminded again why I got up at 5:30 A.M. on Saturday to work nearly for free—care about something enough to share that love with others, and they will care right back. And they will learn. Snowboard pupils ride with their hearts as much as their legs and they succeed when you help them feel bigger than Mt. Rainier.

Lefty

By Pohara Joy S. Heart

*S*cotty stood out amongst the other second graders like the proverbial black sheep. As a new student teacher, I watched him from the back of the classroom, my mind dancing with questions about this cute little boy.

While Mrs. Wagner held the attention of the rest of the class, Scotty often squirmed, fidgeted, crumpled papers, and sporadically mumbled unintelligibly. Several days into my new assignment, it became painfully obvious to me that Scotty had no friends among the other twenty children.

A gentle person and excellent teacher, Mrs. Rosalie Wagner never raised her voice at the children. Instead, she curbed their misbehaviors with a strong look and a quiet: "If you do not stop, I will be very cross with you!" But even that did not often curb Scotty's antsy expressions of frustration.

I learned from Mrs. Wagner that Scotty lived with his single, working mother, which might have explained his discontent, except that out of the twenty-one children in the class, fourteen of them came from broken homes. How could such a small boy be so disruptive to a second-grade class, and more to the point, why?

My heart went out to this child. I knew something about being out of sync, on the fringe and isolated in school, but steeped in my lack of teaching experience, I felt uncertain that I could find a way to help him.

One afternoon, while Mrs. Wagner taught the rudiments of cursive writing, Scotty became particularly agitated. Suddenly I noticed that Scotty was left-handed!

Watching Mrs. Wagner write with her right hand, I realized that this child had no idea how to hold his left hand and write like the rest of the class. Resigned to his inability, he stopped trying to write and let his frustration grow into the all-too-familiar class disturbances.

One thing that I know from my own classroom experiences is that the best teachers are good role models—and Scotty had no role model for left-handed cursive writing! Perhaps there is something I can do after all.

That night, I rummaged through my basement and found a small, ancient chalkboard. Using a stub of chalk, I commenced the challenging task of teaching myself to write left-handed just enough so I could show Scotty how to hold his hand when he wrote.

Over and over again, I tried to form the cursive letters that flowed so easily from my right hand. I practiced and practiced for the next couple of evenings until, at some level, I knew that I had a rudimentary example to offer him.

The next day, when Mrs. Wagner began her penmanship lesson, I called Scotty to the back of the room. "Watch how I hold my hand, Scotty," I said softly, showing him the small chalkboard. With my left hand poised to write, I drafted the same letters that Rosalie was busily forming on the board. Silently, Scotty watched my hand stumble over several curves and loops.

"Are you left-handed?" he asked hopefully, his brows furrowing.

"No," I replied.

"You're not left-handed?" he repeated, eyes wide.

"No, sweetie, I'm not, which means you'll be able to do this much better than I can."

"You mean you're really right-handed?"

"Yes, I am, but you were having difficulty figuring out how to hold your hand, so I taught myself just enough to show you."

He gaped. "You did this for me?"

"Well, yes, of course," I answered. "Because you needed to know how to hold your pencil the way a lefty would."

"You did this for me?" he repeated, his eyes wider than before. "For me?"

I nodded, raw emotion filling my throat, as I watched a look of wonder bloom across his face. Had no one ever done anything special for this child?

Humbly, I continued to instruct him until he seemed to become confident and facile enough in his grip and letter formation to continue on his own. As I watched him tackle his new skill, I sat in awe of what had just occurred.

Obviously the lesson had not been about penmanship at all. The hand and the chalk had been merely a vehicle for something much more profound: A little boy's self-worth—and my own dawning comprehension that teaching may have less to do with skills and more to do with loving.

From that day forward, this feisty little boy began to integrate into the rhythm of the class. He carried himself just a little more confidently, and within a week, he'd found a friend in Chad, another classmate. Though Mrs. Wagner and I still needed to remind him to settle down and do some work, his noises, more often than not, came from his desire to chat with his new friend.

Scotty knew that he had also found an advocate in me. When our class visited the Natural History Museum, he stuck close by with Chad in tow, his small hand clasped tightly in my own.

For the most part, our tender mentor-student relationship flourished harmoniously, but occasionally Scotty tested my patience. One afternoon, while the rest of the children worked on their lessons, Scotty led Chad into a symphony of chatter and giggles. Though their playfulness demonstrated a lot of joy, it still disrupted the classroom.

"Scotty," I admonished him. "Settle down."

Scotty gave Chad a sly glance and giggled more.

"Scotty," I said again. "Stop now and be quiet."

He simply ignored me.

"Scott Johnson," I demanded, "if you do not settle down this minute I will—"

And then I paused, as the possibilities of what I would be willing to carry out flashed across my mind. Of course, I could have him removed from the classroom or put in the corner, but having managed to facilitate his integration into the class, there was no way I would punish him with isolation now.

Time seemed to stand still as I searched my mind for a promise that I could, in loving conscience, back up if he refused to cooperate. Scotty watched me, his eyes wary.

I took one deep breath, and Divine inspiration flooded through my mind. My eyes pierced his as I mustered the sternest expression I could and finished my threat, "—I will be very cross with you!"

Scotty's eyes widened and, in an instant, he had shifted in his seat, picked up his pencil, and busily begun his schoolwork. With a sigh of relief, I returned to the work I'd been doing. Evidently, Scotty must have considered our relationship too precious to risk, for I didn't hear a peep out of him the rest of the day.

Glimpses Beneath the Surface

By Margaret DiCanio

*I*n the late 1960s, I was recruited to teach in a new Head Start Program in Miami. Although I had considerable prior experience working with people who lived in poverty, I had never spent the whole of every working day faced with the body- and soul-numbing impact of too little money. Many of our kids' parents had two and three jobs in order to pay the rent and put food on the table.

Our program divided the kids into two classes, fifteen in the morning, and fifteen in the afternoon. One little girl, Tisha Ann, came to school every afternoon dressed in dainty starched pinafores. More than once, I told her very young mother she should dress her daughter in overalls. In preschool, a day's hard play is likely to accumulate paint, mud, water, and food, not to mention plain old soil picked up while lying on your stomach "reading" a picture book. Her young mother ignored my suggestions.

About three weeks before the school year was to end, Tisha Ann's pregnant mother said, "I can't bring her any more. The clinic doctor says I should stay off my feet as much as possible."

I had two assistants so I was able to say, "I'll come and pick her up during my lunch time." With obvious misgivings, she agreed. One day, because I had another errand, I came a few minutes early.

The little house had no indoor tub. The child sat in a tin tub in the yard with her mother pouring water from a bucket over her. I was sure the doctor had not envisioned the mother hauling water in a bucket from the kitchen sink to the outdoor tub, so I demonstrated what my mother called "a cat wash," washing the child all over with a small basin and a wash cloth.

I groaned at the thought of her washing and ironing the stained pinafores every day. The next day I brought three pairs of seersucker overalls. She blanched when she saw them.

"My neighbors will say I don't take good care of my daughter."

"Tell them I ordered you to dress Tisha Ann in overalls. Tell them if they have questions, I will come to visit them and tell them myself."

For the first time since I'd met her, she grinned. Tisha Ann looked up at her mother and she too grinned. By the end of three weeks, Tisha Ann's overalls were a medley of stains.

Intervening with parents over kids' clothing wasn't all that the job required of me, though. Sometimes more direct action was required. Such was the case with Lamar.

Kids in the morning sessions had a snack halfway through the session and ended with lunch. Kids in the afternoon session began with lunch and had a snack halfway through.

Behaviors among the kids ranged from those who hid behind their mothers to those who would go right out the door and wander around the school. One even dangled by one arm from the balcony of the main building.

Ordinarily Lamar was a sunny little boy. One day he slammed the door as he came in, tipped over a chair, swept the erasers off the blackboard tray, yanked a Raggedy Ann doll away from one of the girls, yanked the hat off a boy playing dress-up, and wound up in front of me. He wrapped both arms tight around my thighs and looked up at me.

"Ain't snack never gonna come?" he said.

With my amazing powers of detection, I said, "Are you hungry?"

His eyes glistened with unshed tears as he nodded.

I pried his arms from around my thighs and retrieved my lunch from the fridge. After he had eaten my sandwich, my cake, and my apple, he was restored to his cherubic self. He probably hadn't eaten since lunch the day before.

I started carrying a bigger lunch and made a pact with Lamar that when he was hungry he would tell me rather than slam the door and knock over a chair, but sometimes his need was so great he forgot.

For me, the most lasting effect I gained from working with my Head Start families was to refrain from rushing to conclusions, especially about people who struggled against such profound odds. Now, if someone's behavior seems odd or counterproductive, I probe gently to find out why. Sometimes it doesn't help. Some people are mired in counterproductive lives. But sometimes, as with Tisha Ann and her mother, they just need an ally. And as with Lamar, sometimes they just need lunch.

"*Research shows . . .*"

By Cindy Lovell Oliver

I always knew I wanted to be a teacher when I grew up. I never agonized over other possibilities. It was a no-brainer. It was recorded in my autobiography, *My Early Days*, written in third grade: *When I grow up I want to be a teacher.* My four younger siblings suffered my attempts to "play school." When their attention waned, I took them on field trips around our farm, mimicking my own classroom teachers. They lined up, alphabetized, broke for lunch, and added sums. I gave directions, assigned homework, read aloud, and graded papers. Our imaginations supplied what the budget did not provide.

Those were the mid-1960s. Easy times. The good old days. Elementary school offered opportunities to excel, to fantasize, and to win spelling bees. How I longed to get up in front of my classmates and take over for my teachers! There was no doubt about it. I would be a teacher someday. But "someday" means different things for different people. Bored in high school, I dropped out, found a job, started my own business, married young, and became "Mom" to Angie first, then Adam. Volunteering in *their* elementary classrooms satisfied my yearning, but just barely. The teachers counted on my creativity, energy, and dedication. The high school dropout became president of the PTA. Life was good. But dreams can't wait.

For anyone who has ever had an epiphany, it will be easy to understand what happened when I had mine. Triggered by a simple poster at a zoo, my first thought was, "Miss So-and-So would love to have *this* in her classroom!" At that same instant an invisible fist slammed into my stomach so hard I barely heard the taunt inside my head: *You're 35 years old, and you'll never be a teacher in your own classroom.* In a daze, my instincts took over. I dialed the local college, and without divulging my name revealed my secret. "Uh, yes, uh, I was just wondering . . . I'm 35 years old, and I want to be a teacher, and, well, I have a GED certificate, so I was curious if there is anything I can do . . . " My voice trailed off as I braced for the onslaught of laughter. Instead I heard, "Oh, yes, we have a teaching program . . . " and I barely heard the details as I allowed myself that first sensation of imagining the fulfillment of my life's dream.

But there were hurdles. A husband who wasn't wild about the idea. The business we owned and operated. A sixty-hour-per-week work schedule. "As long as it doesn't interfere with your work, I don't care how many classes you take!" He didn't think I had it in me. He assumed that one semester would get it out of my system. I told him I would take just one class at a time. But being the first in my family to tackle college, I didn't have the good sense to pace myself, and I signed up for my first ever college classes—seventeen credit hours. There was no time to second-guess myself. Angie and Adam were in high school. Good kids who beamed with pride at their crazy mom going to college in between running the video stores. And in two years and nine months (I didn't know any better!) they beamed even brighter watching me receive my diploma.

The hurdles were gone. That silly piece of paper that kept me from my dream all those years was now in my possession. I was a teacher! Or was I? That was yet to be discovered. The momentum that carried me through college while juggling my "real" job spurred me on. I was hired at my dream school, a tiny school in rural Florida where I often volunteered. I badgered the principal for a key and spent my summer stocking the bookshelves, creating bulletin boards, and writing lesson plans. I arranged and rearranged desks, moved the piano, designed learning centers, and stocked up on supplies. I was ready to teach. And I got my first opportunity before school even started.

Our PTA sponsored a spaghetti dinner on "Meet the Teacher" night the week before classes began. Everyone turned out—not for spaghetti, but to see who their teacher would be. I was delirious. Students—*real* students—would be arriving to meet me, the teacher. I was the teacher! *Their* teacher! I was confident in my training. My classroom was the best. Over 1,000 books lined my newly purchased bookshelves from Wal-Mart. Everyone would want to be in my class! There were board games, puppets, and puzzles. A letter-writing center. An art center. An Author's Chair. No other teacher had an Author's Chair! I would be superb. Suddenly they began to arrive. Tentative. Smiling. Nervous and hopeful, parents approached teachers, extending hands to shake. I knew a few parents from the video store. I even knew some of my students. But some faces were new. *My* face was new. *There's the new teacher . . .* And then it happened: my first test of teaching.

A mother and son approached me. She was eager to please, eager to find her way into my good graces, eager to offer this disclaimer about her son: "Chris has never been a very good student. Ummm . . . " she hesitated, "the teachers have had some problems with him . . . " she fumbled for the right words. My stomach churned. I was no longer the teacher. I was the mom! I knew this feeling . . . I knew her heart. And more importantly, I knew the pained look on Chris's face as he stood in acquiescence. I could have burst into tears on their behalf. What she was trying to say was something I had tried to say to teachers down through the years. Not "he's a handful" or "she's energetic," but the plaintive, *"Please like my child."* And in that instant all of my training gave way to my instincts. Unable to bear another word of confession, I heard myself interrupt her.

Completely winging it, I heard myself say, "Well, research shows . . . " and it was like the old E.F. Hutton commercials when crowds grew silent to hear the famous broker's financial advice. Chris and his mom stood motionless as the calm, assuring, *authoritative* voice continued. "Research shows that boys who have had problems in school, uh, early on, actually do very well when they get to fifth grade. They see themselves as leaders now, you know, the oldest kids in the school, so they, uh, want to set an example and that sort of thing." I prattled on. They hung on every word. Somewhere a little angel's voice—a professor from college (Dr. Dershimer) whispered and coached me. I was paraphrasing her lecture on developmental readiness, but I sure didn't know it at the time. What I did know was that it was having an effect. Chris began to nod, and suddenly he interrupted, turned to his mom, and declared, "I *have* been feeling different lately."

Chris's mom stared in disbelief. So, she seemed to be taking it in, what you're saying is that Chris, my Chris, even though he's had so many problems in school, could suddenly be on the verge of change. Of succeeding. Of being liked by his teacher. All this she said with her face. She believed me.

Totally and completely, she believed me. I was the teacher, after all. The person with credentials. The gatekeeper. I slowly let my breath out. I had survived my first teaching challenge, and school had not even started yet!

I knew about high expectations. We were taught the Pygmalion theory in our education classes. But we were also taught that having high expectations was not enough. We teachers were to provide the support necessary to achieve those expectations. What exactly did that mean? Was I really cut out for this? Only time would tell.

There is nothing—*nothing*—like the first day of school, especially for the beginning teacher. Mine is etched in my memory as the golden moment it was. I'm sure I was nervous, but I only remember the joy. And every day the joy increased. I relied upon my instincts and my training. Following Dr. Dershimer's advice, I made contact with all parents during the second week of school—a phone call home to tell them "something specific and positive—and *not academic!*" about their child. The effect was stunning. One mother burst into tears. "In all these years the only time I ever heard from the school was when he was in trouble." Others seized the opportunity to tell me even more specific and positive tidbits. As a parent myself, I fully understood Dr. Dershimer's advice: Get them in your corner early, so when you need their support, you'll have it.

My students, and Chris in particular, thrived. They, too, were joyful. As I taught and encouraged and celebrated, I tried to gauge success at every level. Yes, there were challenges, but we faced them together. The spirit was one of camaraderie, of teamwork. We honored every accomplishment. And then came the night of the first open house. It was a combination PTA meeting and open house. All day we prepared. Our room was spotless. Organized. Decorated. Best work was proudly displayed. I called, "See you tonight!" as the dismissal bell rang.

At 6:00 we convened in the cafeteria. The room was packed, and the principal directed the teachers to sit at the front. He announced the "class count." Class count! What's this? He began with kindergarten. "Would all the parents, aunts, uncles, etc., from Mrs. Lane's class please stand?" Oh no! It was a competition. I immediately remembered my teacher training. Parents of young children are more interested; as the novelty wears off, so does parental involvement. This was apparently true as the kindergarten and first-grade teachers emerged as top contenders for the teacher with the greatest support. I began strategizing how I would win the class count at the *next* PTA meeting. Third grade, fourth grade, and now the fifth grade supporters were counted. Mrs. Allen was counted first. Yes, involvement had definitely dropped off as the students grew older. But then it was my turn. The sound of dozens of cafeteria chairs grinding on the tile floor was music to my ears. There was a collective intake of breath. Parents, grandparents, aunts, uncles—who were all these people?—stood in support. I had blown the competition out of the water!

That single event stands out in my memory as a great personal triumph, yet I had no idea it would pale in comparison before the night was over. Parents disbursed to the respective classrooms. Students gave their parents the grand tour. I hovered and glided and waltzed 'round the room, smiling and interacting and thanking my wonderful family. And then Chris and his mom came in. Chris began to show her our experiment—we were trying to make coal—and explained the process and why we would never actually see it turn to coal because it would take thousands of years. His animated and detailed account amazed me. We had done the experiment weeks before, and I barely remembered the vocabulary myself. Suddenly his mom turned to me with tears in her eyes. "I just want to look you in the eye and thank you," she whispered. "He's always hated school. He always pretended to be sick. But now he can't wait to come in every day. He hasn't missed a day. His dad and I can't believe it. Thank you for explaining how this year was going to be different." I didn't cry. I didn't speak. I could only smile as Chris interrupted with, "Mom, come and see the poem I wrote."

Not every high school dropout gets to be a teacher. But miracles beget miracles. And Chris was mine.

Story Time

By Hania Rayyan

The boy was out of control, and there was nothing to be done about it.

In fact, everyone at school had said that to me, and after my first encounter with Anas, I myself started to believe it. When I asked him to read a paragraph from the story book I had handed out to the kids in his class, a look of confusion appeared on his face.

He simply said to me, "I do not want to . . ." which amazed me! I was teaching fifth grade that year, and of all the children in my class, it rapidly became apparent that this particular ten-year-old had planned to resist me from the very beginning.

"You might not want to," I said very calmly to him. "But you are going to have to."

He looked at me, astonished, and seemed to be thinking about it for a few seconds. Then he threw his story book on the floor and sighed. I could not believe his nerve. He was actually trying to make me lose my temper.

"Miss Hania, leave him," a quiet girl named Lara informed me. "Or he will start to hit the other kids and throw things at you!"

"Not in my class!" I snapped.

It seemed that my words set him off. As soon as I finished speaking, Anas's face became red with fury. He went up to Lara's seat in the front row, and harshly kicked her in the stomach. Then he threw her books to the floor.

The poor girl cried out in pain. I rushed to the rescue, and helped her to sit down. I made sure that she was all right, then turned to Anas.

He looked proud of what he had done, as if he had defended himself.

I took him by the hand, and tried to lead him outside of the classroom. He resisted, and by that I mean he really resisted me. He was a clumsy boy, but well-built, and quite strong.

I was determined to take him to the principal. I wanted to explain to her what he had done. I didn't want him to think he could ever do such things again (in my class, or in any other).

For her part, the principal had all she could take from that boy. So when she heard what he had done, she pushed him against the wall. Anas hit his head and fell down. I was shocked. I stood there motionless; the boy was not harmed seriously, but was obviously in physical pain. I helped him up. He refused to look at me.

"That was to teach him that there is always someone stronger than you!" the principal told me. "So the next time he thinks of hitting a girl, or anyone else, he has this pain to remember."

She spoke about him with such disgust that I realized I had made a mistake bringing him to her in the first place. I was told to take him back to class. And I did.

I had no idea how to interact with him after what happened. He sat in his place, silent. The other kids were wondering about what the principal did to him, but I did not give them the pleasure of knowing.

All through the lesson, he refused to raise his head. With his book still on the floor, he was just staring at the empty desk in front of him.

The next day, Anas came to me a few minutes after I had entered the fifth-grade classroom. He had his story book in his hand.

"Here is your story book." He had a frown on his face. "Take it back."

"First of all it is not my story book, it is yours. And second, why are you giving it back to me?"

"My dad said to give it back to you. He refused to give me the money to pay you for it."

"Tell your dad that I do not want you to pay for it," I said forcefully. "Tell him it is my gift to you, so that you could learn to read and enjoy the story!" I raised my voice a little, and the other kids heard everything.

"His dad never gives money for anything," one of the other children said.

Anas bristled at the boy who had said it, so I quickly intervened. "Anas, look at me. I do not care if you do not pay for it. I gave this story book to you, and you shall have it."

It was true. I had paid for the books out of my own pocket. When I had told the principal that I wanted to get an interesting story book for the fifth-grade class, she had instructed me to buy the books myself, and collect the money from the kids later.

Anas was ashamed, I could see that in his eyes.

"Go sit in your chair Anas," I told him. "You have no excuse. You've got a story book, and now you are going to read a page from it for us."

He looked at me. The shame in his expression had been replaced by what I took to be poorly hidden satisfaction. Then he took the story book in his hand, sat down, and opened it at the first page.

Anas began to read, but it seemed that he had trouble in reading. He kept blinking his eyes. So I ask him if he forgot his eyeglasses at home.

"He does not have any," another one of the boys said.

By now I was getting irritated by the other kids constantly answering on Anas's behalf. I decided to put a stop to it. "Class," I said to them, "from now on, nobody answers any question for anyone else, only the person asked will do the answering, is that clear?"

"Yes, Miss Hania." They answered in unison.

"So Anas, is there a problem? Do your eyes hurt?"

"No," he said.

"Okay, then, go on reading."

He hesitated for some time, and then finally started again. He would start, say two or three words right, and then the mistakes would begin to creep back in.

I noticed that the words he read correctly were because he was actually looking at the book. The rest must have been him trying to finish the sentence he was reading in his head, rather than continuing to look at it. So at times it just didn't make any sense.

It quickly became clear to me that the boy was very nervous reading in front of the class. The other kids made it harder on him by not sparing his feelings; laughing whenever he made a mistake.

When Anas suddenly stood up, looking for someone to hit, I said: "Anas, sit down please. Class, no one is perfect, we all make mistakes, we will all see that when each of you has your turn to read aloud!" That helped. Anas calmed down, and we got through the rest of the lesson with no more outbursts.

There was another incident where Anas tried to hit a boy on the playground. I happened to be there, and took him aside. I explained to him that he could use strong words more forcefully than his strong arms to defend himself.

At first he seemed to find that idea strange. I knew that this was obviously not what he heard at home, especially from his father.

However, I think I planted that idea in his mind just like a seed. I hoped it would grow. Perhaps I had planted it on that day on the playground when I took him aside. Perhaps it was the time that I took him to the principal's office, and never did so again afterward. Perhaps it was because I gave him the story book when he had no money to pay for it. Perhaps it was any of those times that I tried to show him that I was only interested in him as a person, as a student, as someone I wanted to see do well. I am not sure when it began to occur to Anas that there were other possibilities for him in life. All I know is that it did eventually dawn on him that there were other ways to go through life than the ones he had been choosing up to that point.

I had many talks with Anas that year, since I was not only his English language teacher, but also his art teacher. When it came to art, Anas was very creative, and had many good ideas. He really excelled at it, and that in turn helped to enhance his confidence.

One day when we were working with clay, Anas showed me a pot he had made. This amazed me because Anas never volunteered. I saw that he was taking a risk, and said, "It's very good Anas."

He blushed! Then he said, "Thank you Miss Hania."

Another first! Art was really a way to get through to this boy. From then on I encouraged him whenever I could, and during art time, Anas was allowed to work on whatever he wished. It worked. He began to actually notice good things about his classmates, and art helped him to start fitting in better.

At first his classmates did not like the idea that Anas was really good at anything besides getting furious and hitting others. But Anas was there to remind us all that there is a way to get through to everyone. Thanks to Anas's example, I, the rest of the staff at the school, and especially my fifth-grade students learned this lesson very well that year.

I ran into Anas on the street three years later. By then I was no longer teaching. He ran to me, and came to shake hands with me.

With a big, warm smile on his face, he said: "Miss Hania, do you remember me?"

"Why, of course! Oh, look at you, how much you have grown! What a fine looking teenager you are!"

He was so proud. He had grown taller and lost weight. Most importantly, he seemed so calm and peaceful: so different from the boy I remembered from his first days in my fifth-grade class.

"I still have your story book, Miss Hania," he said to me so proudly. "I read it to my younger brother sometimes!"

I find it hard to describe the feeling I had when I heard this. I felt so warm, so very happy that I was able to get through to the boy, and change something for the better in his life. Anas had learned firsthand the valuable concepts of giving and acceptance, and it had only cost me a few bucks and some well-placed compliments on his artwork.

Library Blues

By David Bara

*D*avid, we'd like to talk with you for a minute." These are not the words a twelve-year-old wants to hear from his sixth-grade teacher and the school librarian. My entire sixth-grade class and I had just trundled in to the library for our weekly hour of browsing, testing our skills in the Dewey Decimal System, and/or reading the book of our choice. My choice was usually something on the space program or astronomy, or science fiction. In fact at that moment I had one of my favorite Scholastic Books tucked under my arm. *Get Off My World!* was sci-fi just the way I liked it, ugly aliens, a youthful hero, a pretty girl, and saviors from an unexpected place; humans who lived miles underground.

I diverted from my usual path to the science section and went to the left in our tiny school library, too small really even for us sixth graders, to where they taught the littlest kids and kindergarteners. Standing there was my teacher, Mr. Wagner, all six feet four of him, and the undertaker-like librarian, Mr. Benner, who sat at his desk.

Mr. Wagner held out his hands to reassure me. "It's okay, son. You haven't done anything wrong. We just wanted to talk to you about the books you've been reading." He seemed concerned. Mr. Benner cleared his throat and chimed in.

"We've noticed that you read an awful lot of science fiction," he said. His voice sounded like the noise my mom's garbage disposal made when she dropped a spoon down it.

"Yeah," I said back. Mr. Benner looked to Mr. Wagner. Wagner crossed his arms and took up the conversation again.

"Well, David, it's just that we think it would be good for you to read something else too, like maybe mysteries or Mark Twain or C. S. Lewis." I tucked *Get Off My World!* ever deeper under my arm. I shuffled my feet and scratched my neck uncomfortably. It was clear they wanted me to respond. At twelve, in front of two such imposing figures, it was hard for me.

"But I like reading science fiction and space stories," I finally said. Now it was the men's turn to shuffle uncomfortably.

"It's just . . . " started Mr. Benner, then stopped. "There's a whole library full of books here, David. We just don't want you to limit yourself to one kind."

I scratched again, playing for time. This was not a subject I wanted to discuss, at all. I just wanted them to let me read what I liked. And there was something about their request that confused me.

Mr. Wagner read my expression. "What is it, David?" he asked gently. He could obviously see this was a touchy subject for me.

"It's just that you read us all those neat books, like *The Prince in Waiting* and *Firestarter* and *Beyond the Burning Lands*. I thought you liked those books," I said to him.

"I do, I do!" said Mr. Wagner. "It's just that we think you could benefit by reading other things too." I stood there for another moment, looking at these two big men who I respected and, yes, feared.

"Okay," I finally said. "What is it you want me to do?"

Mr. Wagner seemed relieved. "Well," he said, rubbing his hands together, "I thought you could start by reading in a group. You're one of our best readers and I thought maybe you'd like work with some other kids in the class?" Actually, I hated that idea, but I was committed and didn't know how to tell them no.

The next thing I knew I was seated at a table with two girls, Leslie Butler and Martha Nelson. Leslie was pretty and had long blond hair and blue eyes, but was painfully shy. Martha was a bit more outspoken, but she was fat and I thought she looked like she would be a nun someday.

So we all sat there staring at each other with *Catcher in the Rye* sitting between us. Actually it was an abridged edition for brilliant young students like us, but I didn't know that.

"I know!" said Martha with far more enthusiasm than I had. "Let's take turns reading a chapter each!" She was bubbly and I hated that.

"A chapter is pretty long. How about we just read a couple of pages each and then pass it along?" I suggested. Leslie nodded at this. I thought that maybe she liked me and would probably go along with whatever I said, so I would always have Martha outvoted.

"Okay then, you go first!" said Martha, sliding the book across the table at me. Ugh. What had I gotten myself into? I thumbed through the first few pages and started reading from Chapter One.

The story started with some kid farting in church, at least that's what I took out of it. Forty-five of the longest minutes later the bell rang and we were off back to our classroom. Forty-five minutes and I hadn't got one page closer to knowing how we were going to beat the Martians. I thought it sucked.

Leslie walked with me all the way back to the classroom. I didn't know what to say to her; I had plenty of trouble talking to girls. She got to her portable and went up the stairs, then stopped and waved to me.

"Bye," she said, smiling.

"Bye," I said back, then watched her go in the door. This was going to be a long Fall.

❈ ❈ ❈ ❈

The next two weeks were just as excruciating. Long dull sections of a book about stuff I really didn't care about. None of it was interesting like the space program, or science fiction stories, or anything like that. The only one who seemed to be enjoying herself was Leslie. She seemed to really like my company, and actually opened up a bit when she read out loud. Martha was her overly cheerful self and me, I was just bored. I was sitting this one out, underachieving as usual, when something miraculous happened.

"David," said Mr. Benner. "Do you have a minute after class?" I snapped up in my chair as if I had been sitting that way the whole time instead of slouching my way out of things again.

"Sure," I said. What was I going to say? I was sure that I had been busted and that now I was going to get in real trouble.

Our session ended and Leslie waved me one last good-bye as I waved back, still oblivious to her obvious charms. I was way too anxious about the trouble I was in.

Mr. Wagner and Mr. Benner stood waiting for me by Mr. Benner's desk. I went up and stood silently, expecting punishment.

"So how do you like *Catcher in the Rye*?" Mr. Wagner asked me.

"It's okay," I lied. Frankly, I found it too complex and boring.

"Well, I was a bit worried it might be too advanced for you. But that's a pretty good edition." Not knowing what to say, I just nodded. This started a long silence.

"You know, you don't have to stay in the group if you don't want to," he said. This sent a spark of life through my whole body.

"I don't?" I said with way too much enthusiasm. Mr. Wagner smiled.

"No you don't. We just wanted you to try something different."

"Well I did, and now I'd like to go back to reading about space," I said. Oh my God! What had I done! I said what I was thinking! What was I thinking?

"Well David," Mr. Benner said. "We'd still like you to read more broadly."

I looked at both men. Mr. Wagner looked on expectantly, while Mr. Benner just had that droll look he always had. The next sentence came out of me before I had a chance to think.

"But this is what I want to read, Mr. Benner. And unless you're telling me I can't, I'm gonna keep reading it." At that point my mind went blank. I was openly challenging the two most important men in my life, telling them what I wanted to do instead of what they wanted.

"I would like you to keep reading other things," said Mr. Benner. I looked up at Wagner, and he just gave me that sideways nod of his. I was going to have to continue to say what was on my own mind, not what I thought these two adults wanted to hear. I looked back at Mr. Benner.

"Isn't it more important that I'm reading, not just that I'm reading something you don't like?" Mr. Benner looked up sheepishly at Wagner, who nodded at me again.

"Go on back to class, David. I'll be along in a minute," he said. I left the library not knowing if I'd won or lost.

At the end of the school day Mr. Wagner came up to me.

"Son," he said, "what you did today was important. It's important that a man decides to stand up for himself. I want you to know that although I don't completely agree with your decision, I respect your right to make it. Just make sure you don't sell yourself short, okay?"

"Okay!" I said, smiling. I knew then that I had won.

That simple experience of being able (at the age of twelve) to tell two grown men what I wanted to read was burned into me. It's the best lesson I ever got in school.

And my first sci-fi novel should be out sometime next year, with luck.

Behind the Veil

By Janet H. Lindemann

*K*im, our junior class counselor, began talking as
soon as I sat down. "Janet,
I want to put a new student, a girl, in one of your honors
classes as soon as she is ready. She's in a mental hospital
right now, but they expect her to be released in a few
weeks. I know it is asking a lot, but I suggested your class.
Her mother has asked if you will write her and start her
on some of the work in your class now."

Kim was one of the best counselors I had known in my
teaching career: sensitive and astute to the needs of students
and teachers. I was teaching five full English classes (three
of them advanced), for a total of 127 students. I knew Kim
would not ask such a favor had she not felt it necessary.

"Of course, Kim," I said. However, the honors classes
were very demanding, designed to challenge the most

capable and disciplined students. We had already covered a great deal. So I asked her, "Do you think she can catch up?"

"She is very bright," Kim said. "But it will be up to her. Her mother wants her to begin to feel she is part of the class now, before she is released."

"How long before she can be in class?" I asked. As much as the course content, I was concerned about Krystal's missing the class experience. Could she fit in? Very bright students could be intimidating and intolerant of what they perceived as lack of ability. Would failure ruin her chances of recovery?

Kim picked up on my hesitation. "We can only do what we can do. Krystal will have to do the rest. Her mother doesn't expect miracles, but she believes Krystal's only chance is to be challenged intellectually."

I admired this mother's courage in risking her daughter's emotional comfort. Protecting her would be so much easier.

I did not bother to ask about the diagnosis of Krystal's illness, and never learned it. Instead, I wrote her a short note:

Dear Krystal,

We are studying *The Scarlet Letter*, by Nathaniel Hawthorne. Your mother is bringing you a copy and study questions to help guide your focus on what the author is saying, and how he forms his meaning. You need to refer to these questions as you read and try to relate them to situations in your own life. Why is the author choosing these incidents and using these characters? Please respond to the questions that seem most important and/or perplexing to you and ask any questions you may have. I want you to be perfectly honest in your responses. Express your questions, frustrations, and disagreements with what the author is writing.

Let me know how else I may help. I am looking forward to meeting you and having you in class.

Sincerely,
Janet Lindemann

Krystal's first reponses came at the end of the week. "So the holy people of Salem had Hester in prison for having a baby with her husband gone. Why didn't they wait for her husband to decide her punishment? Well, adultery was the sin of their society. People are punished today for breaking society's codes, even when the codes are unfair, but the designated sins have changed. Today, being an unmarried mother doesn't seem to matter much, at least not to the mother. I think not having a father matters more to a child than people realize.

"Yes, I noticed the description of the Scarlet A . . . He makes it very beautifully sewn by Hester, herself . . ."

Krystal's honest responses were exactly what I expected from students in my classes. We continued our correspondence about the novel throughout the six weeks. Her questions led me to deeper understanding of this complex novel, and her essay at the end of the six weeks showed maturity and insight both in content and writing style.

I had met Krystal's mother, an intense, intelligent woman who thanked me for my help. She worked full time and came by school weekly to pick up or return the work cycling from the teachers to her daughter. A father was never mentioned. We would chat briefly. She did not seem eager to confide, a fact for which I was glad.

There are parents who sometimes share confidences they should not, enticing a teacher into a role which makes it difficult for that teacher to establish and carry on an objective relationship with the student. I wanted to interact with Krystal in a clearly defined teacher-student relationship. I learned she was due to enter my sixth-period class at the beginning of the second six weeks of the semester.

On the first day of the second six weeks, students gathered in my area, talking and waiting for the tardy bell to signal them to take their seats. We were still in an open-classroom setting, an unfortunate architectural and educational experiment of classrooms without walls. Right before class began, Krystal approached our "room" from the far side of the large, open area that made up our wing.

She was about 5'5", somewhat stocky, and wearing the typical teen costume of jeans, loafers, and white, embroidered, loose tunic. As she walked, she kept her head down, her medium-length curly black hair falling forward, covering her face. She took a seat in the farthermost corner

Teacher Miracles

and scooted the desk back a few feet. She sat, as the other students settled, leaning forward on her hands, her hair continuing to completely shield her face.

The other students cast quick glances in her direction, but did not say anything. I took roll from my seating chart and placed the attendance slip in its envelope on the bookcase dividing my area from the next class. I made a couple of announcements, welcomed them back, and said matter-of-factly, "We have a new student this six weeks, Krystal Meyers. I know you will help her get into the routine."

"Hi, Krystal."

"What routine?"

"Mrs. L is my favorite teacher."

"Still trying for an A, Rob?" The comments drifted in Krystal's direction.

She never moved. I quickly began the class, passing out the reading lists for the six weeks and the week's vocabulary assignment. Brenton, the boy in front of Krystal, leaned way back, then got out of his seat to walk back to hand the papers to Krystal. She took them without looking up.

Days followed pretty much in the same pattern. I usually walked back to hand Krystal's papers to her or to pick up assignments and quizzes. I began to touch her arm or shoulder as I passed. I often had the class write preliminary responses to topics for the day's discussion before oral responses began. I occasionally picked up her writing and glanced at it before putting it back on her desk.

No response from Krystal.

During the second week, Lang, a tall, quiet boy, stopped by my desk after class and asked, "Is she afraid of us? Is there anything I can do?"

"She probably is afraid," I told him. "I think we just have to give her time." He nodded and walked on. I fervently hoped that time was what she needed. I had begun to wonder if she would ever come from behind her veil. I sensed that the students were puzzled, but they kept the distance she had set.

I began inserting Krystal into the discussions. I would say things like, "Krystal had an interesting comment about Twain's use of the river as a symbol." The class would hesitate an instant to glance in her direction. One or two of the girls would comment benevolently, "That's good." But then the day's discussion would continue as if the silent girl were not there.

At the end of the third week, I saw that Krystal's desk was slightly closer to the rest of the class. She was sitting in the desk, so I presumed she had moved it. Was this a breakthrough? As the next weeks passed, gradually her desk got closer until it was in normal proximity to the rest. Also, she was sitting up a little straighter. Her hair still covered most of her face, but a sliver of her chin showed through.

During one very heated class discussion where strong opinions on society's right to force students to go to school were aired, Kent, a stalwart nonconformist, said, "They just want to keep us off the streets. I could learn more without having to be here every day." Krystal silently extended from behind her curtain a note she had been writing. I picked it up and read, "If people couldn't go to school, they would fight to get in. And it would be very easy to spend the money on just the brightest and most powerful."

"Maybe, but . . . " the discussion continued until the bell. Gradually, the changes continued. I would now see Krystal's head nod in agreement or shake in disagreement. She often wrote furiously during discussions and would extend her written comment from time to time. But her hair stayed covering most of her face. The class as a whole treated this as if it were normal behavior.

Students would ask, "What did Krystal write?" or look in her direction. They seemed content to never either see her face, or hear her voice. I worried that this state had become too comfortable, that it offered too easy an escape for her. I was surprised that no one in the class had complained about her special treatment. I did not insist on her participation or challenge her statements as I did with the other students. I did not push her by saying things like, "You have to give better examples than those to convince me," or "that is too easy, what if . . . ?" Was I taking the easy way out? I was afraid of a setback if I made demands too soon. Maybe this was the best we could hope for.

Near the end of the six weeks, the class was discussing the nature of evil. I had gone out on a limb in suggesting the subject, but felt that the students needed to clarify for themselves their ideas. The nature of evil has been the theme of much, if not all, great literature. I had asked the class to suggest an undeniable act of evil. Of course, murder had been named with the ensuing arguments: "Is it always evil? What if . . . ? Who decides . . . ? What if a person doesn't know any better?"

At one point a boy named Trenton said, in frustration, "How can we know, and if we don't know, why should we care?"

Lisa, my staunch church member and Bible scholar, said, "Even if we don't know for sure if something is evil, we can't just do anything we feel like. That is going back to the jungle. God created us to be above the animals."

"I don't even know if there is such a thing as evil," Trenton shot back. "If it is all relative then it depends on when you are born, and where." Abruptly he turned to the back of the "room" and said, "I want to hear what Krystal thinks."

The class got quiet. Krystal quit writing and raised her head. She deliberately brushed her hair aside and tucked it behind her ear. She looked at Trenton levelly and calmly. "Evil is real. I don't know all that it is, or why it is, but I have felt it. I knew it."

"What do you mean?" a girl named Paula asked, "by 'felt it'?"

"It is being lost from everyone, and no one cares. It is feeling hateful to someone or everyone and you don't care. It is being afraid nothing will ever be good again."

"But doesn't someone cause it?" Lisa said. "Isn't that what makes it evil?"

As the discussion continued, I noted Krystal's deep black eyes, saw her head nodding, heard her saying little, but she was no longer behind her veil. She never retreated behind it again.

No one person or thing brought about Krystal's change. A miracle grew in that space, for that girl, because we allowed it. It grew out of the respect and patience with which the class enveloped Krystal; out of her mother's courage and determination; out of the fact that I had accrued enough experience to allow her to evolve within her own magnificent intellect and spirit; and it grew from a fellow student who had the honesty, courage, and intuition to ask her to join him in the world as a full participant.

Better Late Than Never

By Mimi Greenwood Knight

*Y*ou only think you appreciate an outstanding teacher when you have children who are ahead of the pack, kids who learn easily. But when you watch your child struggle and lag behind, when you cry and pray and wait for him to catch up, that's when you need the teacher of a lifetime. My family was blessed with two of these rare jewels, Sharron Curole and Susie Tosso.

Our first two children were girls, girls who knew their ABCs before they started school, who devoured everything they learned in kindergarten, who spoke the Queen's English at three. During those years, I was quick to tell my friends with more "normal" children, "Don't worry. All kids develop at their own pace. Give him time. Don't rush him."

Then came our third child and time for me to eat my words. Hewson was the original "Leo the Late Bloomer." He did everything late. Not just later than his sisters, but later than all the other kids we knew. I promised myself I wouldn't pull out the girls' baby books and compare. Then I would and I'd panic at all the stuff he wasn't doing.

Breastfeeding was a test of endurance, 45 minutes at a sitting. Even when I caved and put him on formula, a bottle took twenty minutes to drink. When it was time for baby food, he didn't seem to "get" the spoon. I'd work it into his mouth and three-fourths of the food would come sloshing back out. I'd complain to my friends about it, and hear my own words coming back at me, "Relax! He'll do it when he's ready. Give him time." Had it sounded that callous when I said it?

Large motor skills were definitely Hewson's thing. He crawled and walked on target but we thought he'd never talk. While his sisters could hold an intelligible conversation at two, Hewson said "Da-Da" and "Ma-Ma" and not much else. At three he could name his family and a few foods but didn't care to say much more. He was taking no prisoners with his large motors though, trying things his sisters never would. He tore around our deck on his Big Wheels, crawled up and jumped off anything that stood still, ensuring job security for the emergency room staff.

He was three and a half before he really spoke. One day after we'd watched *George of the Jungle*, he went out to the swing set, took a headlong run, flung himself across the swing on his belly, and sang out, "George a'Jungle watch a'tree!"

Half an hour later, I heard crying in the playroom. I found my oldest sobbing and Hewson, fists planted defiantly on his hips, explained, "She hit me. I hit she!" That was that. When Dad got home that night, Hewson was talking.

In a house full of bookworms, he showed little interest in books beyond stacking them up to climb on and get things out of reach. His sisters had sat for hours as I read mountains of books. The only time Hewson stayed still was when he slept, ate, or bathed. So I took to reading to him in the bathtub and high chair where every so often he'd glance up, half interested in the pictures.

We won't even talk about potty training. Suffice it to say I started to wonder if maybe some kids do go off to college in diapers. But in true Hewson fashion, once he decided he was ready to tackle the potty, he went from Pampers to Spider-Man undies in one afternoon.

A blink of the eye and it was time for school, and the real worrying began. From day one Hewson loved kindergarten. He couldn't get enough of the other boys on the playground and quickly emerged as a leader. The classroom, though, was another story. Weeks turned into months as the other kids learned their numbers and letters and Hewson could barely write his name. My husband, David, and I were basket cases, but Mrs. Curole didn't seem concerned.

She praised Hewson for the things he did well and helped him to see school as a good place to be. He adored her and couldn't get out of bed fast enough on school days.

I started volunteering in the classroom, peeking over shoulders as the other kids carved out perfect little 5s and Bs. I walked the halls looking at their artwork, precise little stick people with a yellow ball sun in one corner and their name carefully lettered underneath. Then I'd spot Hewson's indecipherable scribbles and my belly would ache.

I read somewhere that boys prefer nonfiction, so I bought books on dinosaurs, cars, animals, fishing, highway construction. He loved sports so I spent hours sitting by the side of the tub reading painfully dry books of football stats and baseball records. At least he was paying attention now. We requested frequent conferences with Mrs. Curole where she'd assure us, "Boys often develop later. Give him time." Hey, that's my line.

Towards the end of the year, though, she recommended Hewson go on to transitional first grade, "to give him a little more time." David was a hard sell but finally agreed that's what we'd do. Kindergarten graduation came and Hewson was the only child who didn't know his letters or numbers. More reassurance from Mrs. Curole and we were on to transitional first grade, where the baton was passed to Mrs. Tosso. She told us success stories of other kids who'd been through her classroom. She talked about "that little light" going on and told us it would happen when it happened. I just hoped it was before Hewson's self-esteem hit the pavement.

I spent his first hour of T-1 crouched down in the hallway peeking at him through the keyhole and went home to report to David that Mrs. Tosso was another answer to our prayers.

Still we prayed and worried, worried and prayed. We requested he be tested for learning disabilities. He loved the testing because the teacher gave him candy. After four months, we heard the words we'd come to hate. "He's a late bloomer. He just needs time." Tell it to somebody else's parents.

I bought him a copy of *Leo, the Late Bloomer* and sat by the side of the tub reading it along with more boring sports stats and a book he loved about the Titanic. Fast forward to spring when an amazing thing happened. After eight months in T-1, that elusive little light in Hewson's head came on one day—just like everybody said it would. It's like he woke up, rubbed his eyes, and for the first time noticed these things around him called letters and numbers. It reminded me of the day I got my first pair of glasses and realized I could see the leaves on the trees and the individual blades of grass.

From March to the end of school, he went from learning his alphabet to sounding out words. It was "George a'Jungle" all over again, or like watching a time-lapsed film of a flower opening. One day we were riding down the road and he read out a sign that said, "LOG HOMES." I cried so hard I couldn't see the road.

At the end-of-school awards ceremony, Mrs. Tosso awarded Hewson the Most Improved Student award. Afterward she and David and I stood in the hall outside his classroom and cried. That was two years ago. I saw Mrs. Tosso in that hallway again the other day, where she and I stared at a list of all the books the second graders had read that year. Hewson was ahead of the other kids by a hundred books. There aren't words to thank someone for that.

There's a saying I love, "Who takes a child by the hand takes a parent by the heart." That was certainly our experience. Mrs. Curole and Mrs. Tosso are both retiring this year. They leave behind them a legacy of children who were loved for who they are, who were afforded the freedom to be themselves and the inspiration to become the best selves they could be. It's not often you find a person who's doing the exact job they were born to do. When you do, it is a miracle to witness.

Victor

By Maria Aldecoa, as told to Agie Pascua

*I*n the late '60s, my monthly salary as an English teacher in the Philippines was roughly equivalent to what today's minimum wage earner would earn in an hour. So no one was really surprised when, after ten years in the classroom, I finally decided to sell insurance full-time. After all, I also dreamed of giving my children a comfortable life.

Apart from financial considerations, however, I never would have thought of leaving academia. I looked forward every day to sharing the best of world literature with 300 sixteen-year-old boys, all high school seniors in Manila's oldest Catholic university. As advisor of the high school literary organ, I took great pleasure in reading sincere attempts at creative writing, many of which transcended sophomoric levels and indicated a brilliant future for these writers in the world of letters.

My greatest fulfillment, however, was in playing second mother to these boys, especially those in my advisory class. While I certainly did not tolerate any hanky-panky, they knew that I could see through a devil-may-care veneer, and help the fallen angel underneath.

Such was the case with Victor, who had come to our humble institution from an exclusive boys' school, apparently as an accommodation to his senator-father. (It was our policy not to accept transferees.)

Victor was quite likeable and low-key. He never wore his pedigree like a dog tag, and I never saw him strut his stuff.

Actually, I hardly saw him at all. He averaged about two absences a week, and always missed my regular Friday quizzes. When he was in class, he was either daydreaming or casting furtive glances at a pretty young miss who always waited for him outside the school building at the close of class hours. (Our classroom had windows that opened out to the street.) As the first grading period neared its end, I had very little basis on which to rate his class standing.

Repeatedly calling his attention to this had obviously not worked. It was time for a long, after-hours talk.

He apologized for his habitual absences, both physical and mental, but volunteered no explanation.

"Does your girlfriend have anything to do with it?" I asked, tempted to attribute the problem straightaway to foolhardy young love.

"She's not my girlfriend, Ma'am." He kept his gaze down, as if counting the specks of dust on his shoes.

Before I could sigh with relief, he quickly added, "She's my wife."

Instantly I was inside the confessional. He was going to be a father in six months. Their parents had almost disowned them. His father the senator, while deeply disappointed, could not accept that his first grandchild would be illegitimate. So Victor and Debby had been married—in very simple rites, with only their most intimate friends and family members in attendance.

Victor sat trembling beside me. He was sixteen going on sixty.

I thought of my own children, then aged ten, eight, and three. Sometimes I wish they would remain kids forever. But that would mean I hadn't grown up, myself.

I took my student's hand in mine. This was no time for recriminations. The only way to go was forward, and I told him so.

"Like it or not, you're going to be head of a family. And you can't be a good provider without a good source of income. You can't rely on your parents forever, and you shouldn't. That's why they send you to school. And that's why you should learn all you can—to prepare yourself for the future."

His frequent absences had taken a toll on his class performance, in almost all subjects. It would be very difficult for him to catch up, especially with the added responsibility of impending fatherhood, for which he was totally unprepared. I advised him to drop out of school for a year and concentrate on his current personal responsibilities.

"But be sure to re-enroll next year," I reminded him. "You still have a long way to go."

He did. And he has come a long way, literally and figuratively. I accidentally bumped into him some fifteen years ago in Chicago, which has been our place of residence since the early '80s. Victor is now a successful physician. He is, in fact, a member of the medical team that is helping me battle cervical cancer—and adamantly refuses to accept any payment.

"No one lets his former teacher pay," he says. "It would be like charging his own mother."

I lie still, every day in the radiation room, waiting for the Lord to heal me completely. As I benefit from the scientific and technological breakthroughs of this era, I am grateful for the never-ending miracles that spring from continuous discovery and education. And once again, I feel proud to have been a teacher, even for only ten years.

Somewhere, my 3,000 boys are performing more miracles. In their own unique ways, they are helping the world turn. And I am honored to have been a part of their lives.

About the Contributors

Maria Aldecoa ("Victor") has written a regular cooking column for the *Community Builder*, a publication for the Filipino community in Chicago.

Julie T. Anderson ("Why I Did It") lives in Berkeley, California, where she teaches high school English.

Cassandra W. Andre ("Orange Hair") is working on a children's picture book about depression.

Jan Baker ("Langston Learns to Write") is retired in Mexico after thirty years of teaching English.

David Bara ("Library Blues") has been writing fiction for more than twenty years in Auburn, Washington.

Melissa S. Bennett ("Wake-Up Call") spent several years teaching art, advanced art, and English as a Second Language at the middle school level in Pennsylvania.

Derringer Award-winning mystery writer Michael Bracken ("Write What You Know") is the author of eleven books. He lives in Waco, Texas.

Barbara W. Campbell ("Music for Life") writes short stories, nonfiction memoirs, and articles which have appeared in *Australian Woman's Weekly*.

Domenico Capilongo ("Empty Hand, Empty Mind") lives in Toronto, Canada, and teaches high school creative writing and alternative education.

Anna Cody ("Embarrassment") is a teacher, short story writer, and mom.

Josh Cox ("It's All Inside") is a graduate student in the creative writing M.F.A. program at Pennsylvania State University.

Margaret DiCanio ("Glimpses Beneath the Surface") is a freelance writer, a sociologist, and a psychologist, who has written the monthly newsletter for the New England Chapter of Mystery Writers of America.

Elizabeth Eidlitz ("Sure Things") is a freelance writer, editor, and columnist for the *Metrowest Daily News*.

Lawrence D. Elliott ("She Gently Opened Doors") is a Realtor® located in Southern California.

Anne Forbes ("Saving a Life") has a bachelor's in English education, a master's in Library Science, and a master's in Computer Science.

Marianne Forkin ("Tales from the Best Music Teacher in the Universe!") is a Berklee College of Music Graduate who is currently teaching general classroom music/band to elementary and junior high students at various schools in Northeastern Pennsylvania.

Marcia Gabet ("Modern Magic") is a retired veteran of thirty years of teaching in a primary classroom. She lives in a rural community with many Amish neighbors and friends.

Joyce Grant-Smith ("Seeing Through Tom") is a sixth-grade teacher in Annapolis Royal, Nova Scotia.

Dianna Graveman ("Goodwill Cranes") currently teaches college writing for the University of Phoenix at the St. Louis campuses.

Jo E. Gray ("Enrichment") is a former elementary school teacher –having served twenty-three years in the public school system.

Mimi Greenwood Knight ("Better Late Than Never") is a freelance writer and artist-in-residence living in South Louisiana.

Patricia Harrington, M.Ed. ("Who Learned More?"), was an elementary school teacher in the Tacoma School District, and is currently is a grant writer and author.

Pohara Joy S. Heart, M.A. ("Lefty"), a published poet, journalistic feature writer, and business copywriter, has held positions on several Colorado publications.

Joel Thomas Hoffschneider ("Ten-Minute Tommy and the Seven-Minute Mile") has been in education for nineteen years. His teaching career has taken him from (East) Los Angeles, California, to Indiana, where he resides.

Carol Kilgore ("Life in Twenty-Five Easy Lessons") currently lives in Corpus Christi, Texas and is the author of thirty published stories.

Lancer Kind ("Bigger Than Mt. Rainier") has taught skiing in Montana, Colorado, and Washington. When he isn't busy in the snow, he's working on one of his science fiction novels.

Dona J. Kirby ("Learning to Read as a Late Bloomer in Oregon") is a Special Education teacher in the Kent, Washington, School District.

Originally from Utah, **Kevin Klein** ("Staying Gold") is now a teacher in Perth, Australia.

Janet H. Lindemann ("Behind the Veil") is a retired English teacher of over twenty years' experience.

Tab Lloyd ("His Story") has enjoyed working with students with special needs for over ten years.

Natalie Lorenzi ("Of Magellan and the Bottom of the World") is an ESOL teaching specialist (English for Speakers of Other Languages) and has taught in Italy, Japan, and Virginia. She lives in Trieste, Italy, with her husband and three children.

Cindy Lovell Oliver ("'Research Shows . . .'") is a professor at her alma mater, Stetson University, in DeLand, Florida, where she directs the HATS (High Achieving Talented Students) Program.

Catherine K. March ("I Love You, Too, Charlie") lives on the shores of beautiful Lake Erie, where she provides consulting services to local school districts and pursues her lifelong love, writing.

Alexis Munier ("Dancing for Dolmen") is an American ex-pat writer, teacher, and opera singer based in Lausanne, Switzerland.

Kenneth Pobo ("Returning") teaches English and Creative Writing at Widener University in Chester, Pennsylvania.

Sarah Raymond ("Giving Birth") has taught art in public galleries, community centers, and high schools in Ontario, Canada.

Hania Rayyan ("Story Time") is a freelance journalist who is working from home in Jerusalem.

Kathleen Reif-Burke ("Star Student") teaches writing from time to time at Keiser College in Port St. Lucie, Florida.

Kyle Richtig ("A Dream Fulfilled") cofounded the magazine *Inscribed* in 2005, and is one of the editors.

Jacqueline Seewald ("A Student to Remember") has written short stories, poems, essays, reviews, and articles that have appeared in numerous publications such as: *The Christian Science Monitor*, *Library Journal*, and *Publishers Weekly*.

For thirteen years **Amy Shore** ("Friends, Romans, Countrymen!") taught English in a number schools, and currently lives in Houston, Texas.

Cristy Trandahl ("Sammi's Priceless Popsicle Stick") works as a freelance writer and lives in rural Minnesota.

Carol Zook ("Mr. Never Give Up") recently retired from a thirty-four-year teaching career. She lives in Fort Wayne, Indiana, with her husband.

Acknowledgments

THERE ARE SO MANY people who deserve an acknowledgement for playing a part in the making of this book, that I scarcely know where to begin. I suppose the best place to start would be with the "talent."

So let me commence by thanking all of the authors whose work you find between these covers. It has been my considerable privilege to get to know them, to work with them, and in the most interesting and unexpected ways, to learn from them. Thanks a lot, gang. You've got my number. Don't be strangers.

Next, I'd like to thank a few of the teachers who made a difference in my own life: my parents, my brother, my extended family and friends, and of course, wonderful educators like Mrs. Delores Sanborn, Mr. Jerry Prescott, Mr. John Traynor, Mr. Daryl Isotalo, Professor Richard W. Donley, Dr. Claude Nichols, Dr. Martin Seedorf, Dr. Mike Green, Dr. Russ Hubbard, Dr. Robert Carricker, and

Dr. Stephen Balzarini. I'm positive that I didn't thank you nearly enough at the moments when it might have counted most, so let me say it now, either for the first time, or for the next time: thanks for your help. I will never forget you.

I'd also like to thank my old friend Paula Munier for believing that I could take on a project this large and coordinate it (and more to the point, for convincing *me* that I could!). And then there's the rest of that wonderful, supportive group there at Adams Media: Brendan O'Neill and Andrea Norville. Thanks for your flexibility, for your professionalism, and for your patience. It has been my sincere pleasure to work with you.

Lastly, let me thank you, the reader, for providing both reason and audience for us to share these stories with you.

About the Editor

Brian Thornton ("Coochie") is the author of *101 Things You Didn't Know about Lincoln*, *The Everything® Kids' States Book*, and *The Everything® Kids' Presidents Book*. His short stories and essays have appeared in *Alfred Hitchcock's Mystery Magazine*, *Bullet(UK)*, *Shred of Evidence*, *Columbia: the Magazine of Northwest History*, and *The Pacific Northwest Forum*. He has a B.A. in history from Gonzaga University and an M.A. (also in history) from Eastern Washington University. He lives and teaches in Seattle, Washington.

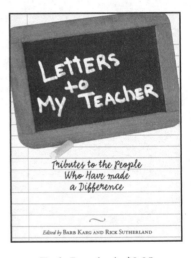